LIFE IN THE SPIRIT

The Life God Always Intended You to Live

J.R. Polhemus

Life In The Spirit
The Life God Always Intended You For You To Live
by J.R. Polhemus

Printed in the United States of America.

ISBN 9781498486941
ISBN (Kindle): 9781498486958

To contact the author:
jr@therock.org
www.jrpolhemus.com

www.xulonpress.com

Dedications

To my incredible family: Yvonne, Mike and Anna…I would not have made it without your love and support!

Acknowledgements

I am very grateful to Alicyn Amann, Sally Wood, and first and foremost my incredible personal assistant, Jan Fennema. Your hours of help, made this book possible. Also thanks to Wendy K. Walters, my editor who went the extra mile in doing a great job.

What leaders are saying...

In his new book, *Life in the Spirit*, J.R. Polhemus shares his journey from the depths of despair to a place of peace, joy and power in the Holy Spirit. J.R.'s insights are inspiring, his stories are gripping, and his research is compelling. Yet *Life in the Spirit* is more than a theological study or a collection of exciting stories, it's a training manual filled with wisdom, written from the front lines of the battlefield of life. You won't want to miss this book!

Kris Vallotton

Senior Associate Leader, Bethel Church, Redding, CA
Co-Founder of Bethel School of Supernatural Ministry
Author of eleven books, including
The Supernatural Ways of Royalty and *Spirit Wars*

Life in the Spirit invites readers to live adventurously and climb to new heights in their faith. My friend J.R. will challenge and transform your perspective on what it means to follow the Holy Spirit. If you desire to deepen your relationship with Holy Spirit, this book is for you!

John Bevere
Author, Minister
Messenger International

I have always enjoyed my engagement with The Rock Church in Castle Rock, Colorado and, in particular, my conversations with J.R. He understands the Father's wishes that we seek the Kingdom and Jesus builds the church. The Holy Spirit is essential to that dynamic. Leaving out the incomparable genius of the Holy Spirit is bad news for our congregations and awful news for the world around us. Only His power to transform lives can enable us to succeed in the ministry of God's Kingdom on earth.

J.R. is a leader, filled with the Spirit, who enjoys a wide-eyed sense of wonder about the Lord and His Kingdom. It shows up in how he speaks, acts and leads. I love his honesty in this book. We should all share stories of our needs, failings and growth opportunities created in us by the beauty and power of the Holy Spirit.

I love the Spirit of God. Reading *Life in the Spirit* will empower you to love Him too. It will create a hunger and desire in you to learn how to simply walk hand in hand with this awesome, astonishing Person who is beloved among the Three and adored in Heaven and Earth.

Graham Cooke
Author, Speaker, Consultant

I have known J.R. for 10 years. He has traveled with me, and together with Bill Johnson and Leif Hetland, we have conducted two healing conferences at his church (The Rock). He has served as an advisor for me. His book, *Life in the Spirit*, explains clearly and practically how to flow with the Holy Spirit in every area of life. His passion to pursue God, love Jesus, and explore the power of the Holy Spirit jumps off the pages. You will be personally impacted by this book. Enjoy the many stories which demonstrate how the Holy Spirit is still operating today through all of us.

Randy Clark, D. Min, Ph.D.
Overseer of Apostolic Network
Global Awakening

As a student and teacher of how God sounds, I am repeatedly asked one question, "How can I hear God better for myself and others?" My consistent reply is, "Develop a deeper relationship with the Holy Spirit." *Life in the Spirit*, like its author J.R. Polhemus, is both relationally authentic and theologically rock-solid. This book carries great truth, but more importantly it is about a truthful experience with the one Jesus calls "the Spirit of Truth." I encourage every truth seeker to read this book. It will change your life.

Bob Hazlett
International Speaker, Prophetic Minister
Author, *The Roar: God's Sound in a Raging World*

The twists and turns of J.R. Polhemus' journey alone are worth reading *Life in the Spirit*. But he has gone on and done an excellent job with walking us through understanding the actual person of the Holy Spirit as well as recognizing the great need in our lives for a deep relationship with Him. Don't miss this!

Robby Dawkins
International Bestselling Author and Conference Speaker

My favorite thing about J.R. is his love for all God's children. You may find it strange to hear, "I love you a lot," just minutes after meeting him for the first time. But how much closer would we be as a civilization if we lived this way. We are all God's children, which makes us brothers and sisters in Christ. So why shouldn't we love everyone like this? My family and I have attended The Rock church in Castle Rock for the past few years and there is true community and family. This was God's plan for us with the church.

Reading *Life in the Spirit* will bring you closer to what God intended you, His child, to be.

Britton Colquitt

NFL Punter, 2016 Super Bowl Champion Denver Broncos

Pastor J.R. is the real deal! Not only will you find this book to be engaging, but more importantly, you will walk away with a deeper understanding of who the Holy Spirit is and what the Holy Spirit does in our daily living. Pastor J.R.'s insights are helpful and easily applied from the rich backdrop of his diverse experiences in life. Don't miss *Life in the Spirit!*

Sarah Hickey Bowling

International Author, Speaker, Pastor

J.R. is a regular speaker in our YWAM schools in Colorado. He has a powerful way of ministering to our staff and students and moves in the things of the Spirit with great ease and sensitivity. I've known him for over twenty years and can say without a doubt that he is a man who lives what he preaches. *Life in the Spirit* contains teaching and stories that will change your life!

Peter Warren

Director YWAM Denver

It's not normal for an editor to give an endorsement for a book. All the other endorsements have come from people who have known and served with J.R. for many years, some for decades. I'm different. I know him only through the pages of this remarkable book. Through ink alone I have borne witness to his spirit and recognized the Spirit of God alive in his heart. Through his vulnerability, I believe you will find your victory. *Life in the Spirit* will ignite a new hunger in you to know the Person of the Holy Spirit.

Wendy K. Walters
Editor, *Life in the Spirit*
Motivational Speaker, Bestselling Author, Ghostwriter

Before we moved to Castle Rock, Colorado, a well known speaker exhorted me to attend "The Rock" and meet the pastor of this growing church. From the moment I encountered J.R., I experienced a loving, kind, hospitable and genuine man who was dialed into the life of the Holy Spirit. If you want to learn practical insights on living and walking in the Spirit, look no further. In *Life in the Spirit*, J.R. walks us through a host of living stories that will bring transformation to your life in the Spirit.

Dave Gustaveson
Former Leader of YWAM Colorado

J.R. has been a close friend of mine for over 20 years. His love for God and intimacy with the Holy Spirit has greatly impacted my life and ministry. I believe *Life in the Spirit* will not only encourage you to build a closer relationship with the Holy Spirit, but will clear up much misunderstanding. There is an impartation that comes from *Life in the Spirit* which will change your life and help others as well. Enjoy!

Pastor George Morrison
International Speaker and Leader
Senior Pastor, Faith Bible Chapel

I have known J.R. Polhemus and his wonderful wife, Yvonne, for many years. Every time I minister at the Rock, there is an open Heaven and a power explosion of God's Holy Spirit. I always wondered why, and now I know—they always make room for the Holy Spirit of God to move freely, revealing Jesus and who He is. *Life in the Spirit* will help you to understand also and change your life. It has opened my eyes to much more of how the Holy Spirit leads, guides, and comforts us through this life.

Shirley L. Strand President, Wind Of The Spirit Ministries
Colorado Springs, Colorado

After a turbulent start to his life, J.R. has emerged from the redemptive journey as a spiritual father, in love with the Holy Spirit, and no one can seem to get him to change the subject! In *Life in the Spirit* you will undoubtedly receive hope, encouragement and an impartation as many of us have who have been impacted by his life and ministry.

Jon Petersen
International Speaker
24-7 Prayer/Boiler Room Network Oversight

J.R. Polhemus

LIFE IN THE SPIRIT

"The Life God Always Intended You To Live"

Table of Contents

Title Page i
Copyright Page ii
Dedications v
Acknowledgements vii

FOREWORD **By Leif Hetland . . . . xvii**
SECTION ONE **Life in the Fast Lane 19**
1 The Search Begins 21
2 Seeking to Find God 25
3 The Next Step 30
SECTION TWO **An Important Role of the Holy Spirit 37**
4 Addicted and Changed 39
SECTION THREE **The Empowering of the Holy Spirit . . . 45**
5 How Can We Make a Difference in This World 47
6 Do People See Jesus in You? 57
SECTION FOUR **The Gifts of the Spirit 69**
7 Meant for Today 71
8 The Revelation Gifts 78
9 The Power Gifts 84
10 The Verbal Gifts 90

SECTION FIVE **Impartation by the Spirit 101**

11 How the Holy Spirit Communicates With Us. 103

12 Put to The Test 113

13 The Power of Love 126

SECTION SIX **Healing of the Body 133**

14 Does God Still Heal? 135

15 Old Covenant or New? 145

16 There's More Than One Way to Be Healed 154

SECTION SEVEN **Healing of The Emotions 163**

17 Emotional and Physical Healing. 165

18 Destiny's Enemy. 173

19 The Keys to Being Set Free 182

SECTION EIGHT **Speaking or Praying in Tongues 195**

20 The Full Spectrum of Beliefs 197

21 Exploring the Mystery 214

SECTION NINE **The Comforter 225**

22 The Comforting Role of The Holy Spirit. 227

23 He is Working All Things For Your Good 236

AFTERWORD Afterword 243

Endorsement 243

FOREWORD

"No eye has seen, no ear has heard, and no mind has imagined what God has prepared for those who love Him.' (1 Cor 2:9 NLT)

My journey with J.R. Polhemus began ten years ago when my friends Randy Clark and Bill Johnson invited me to do a healing conference at the Rock Church in Castle Rock, Colorado. The greatest joy for me was to connect in a covenant relationship with J.R. and Yvonne who, as lead pastors, were guiding a church impacting the community and nations with power and love.

When I experience a culture that is influencing culture, I love to know the story behind the story. If the Rock Church was a restaurant and J.R. was the master chef, I would want to know the secret within their special sauce. *Life in The Spirit* is written for anyone who has a desire for more. At a time of great need in personal and public life, God is sending a widespread move of His Holy Spirit. The Holy Spirit is looking for sons and daughters who will partner with Him to see the supernatural become natural.

While many believers have experienced a baptism in the Holy Spirit, they have allowed the event of baptism to be the defining moment rather than focusing on the need for a life-long relationship with the person of the Holy Spirit. Born of the Spirit, filled with the Spirit and walking in the Spirit are the keys to touching heaven and transforming earth.

One of the scripture verses that stretch me for the more is "As He is, so are we in the world" (1 John 4:17b NLT). For me, this verse changes everything. Each one of us as Spirit-filled sons and daughters is one with His victory over death, hell and the grave. Therefore, His victory is mine in every area of life–in this world and the next. I am one with Him in His authority; therefore, all things are under my feet because they are under His feet.

It is time to wake up to another world that can only be experienced with a life in the Spirit. The greatest gift J.R. Polhemus has been in my life as a friend is one who is a great friend of the Holy Spirit. When the Holy Spirit controls our lives, He produces this kind of fruit in us: love, joy, peace, patience, kindness, goodness, faithfulness, gentleness and self control. (Gal 5:22-23).

J.R. has been by my side on several trips into the darkest places of the world. When you get squeezed, what is in you comes out. The author has been squeezed and the result has been the character and competence of Jesus that only the Holy Spirit can produce. Now a *Life in The Spirit* is available to all of us through this life-changing book.

It is time to surrender your life from ordinary to extraordinary! Rest in His life and find life in the Holy Spirit!

Leif Hetland
Founder and President, Global Mission Awareness
Author of *Seeing Through Heaven's Eyes* and *Healing The Orphan Spirit*

Section 1

LIFE IN THE FAST LANE

"All truths are easy to understand once they are discovered; the point is to discover them."
- Galileo Galilei

When you are searching for something you do not understand and cannot describe, the path is anything but clear. It wanders, sometimes aimlessly, yet the pull towards that something keeps you searching and hungry. You cannot stop until you have tasted and seen.

Chapter 1:

The Search Begins

I could hear the siren blaring as it got closer and closer to our home. Then the vehicle stopped. Red lights were flashing as men dressed in white hurriedly entered our home. At 4-1/2 years old I knew the excitement was all about me. Hands lifted my limp frame onto a stretcher. Someone thrust a plastic oxygen tent over my body. The attendants hustled me into the ambulance. Off we sped to the hospital in Trenton, New Jersey about a ten mile trip from my home in eastern Pennsylvania. As we hurried down the road, I gasped for breath. When I looked up I saw the concerned face of Dr. Hiner, our family physician.

Suddenly, without warning everything went dark, very dark: No sounds, no light, and no commotion, just darkness. I remember sensing complete peace; a peace so profound I struggle to describe it. Next I saw a man surrounded by bright, white light. The peace I felt was out of this world. "*Where am I?*" I wondered. I felt disoriented but still at peace as I saw a spectrum of extremely vivid colors.

Then the man spoke; "*You need to go back.*" His caring eyes were like pools of deep love.

"I don't want to leave," I thought.

Suddenly, I was back in the ambulance. Many faces etched with concern stared down at me. Later my mother said to me, "Wasn't it wonderful how Dr. Hiner brought you back to life?"

"Mom, it wasn't him," I replied. "It was Jesus."

At the time this puzzled my mother, but throughout my childhood she often repeated this story back to me. She always made sure to emphasize my response. Somehow, I *just knew* the man I had seen in the ambulance that night was someone worth knowing more intimately.

This was my first journey into the realm of the Spirit. This glimpse into heaven still amazes me. However, as I grew up and continued to struggle with asthma, the reality of this experience faded into the recesses of my memory. Still, I felt closer to God after this experience. The year after it happened, I remember sitting by our home on the Delaware River bank thinking; *I know God has a reason for my being here on earth.*

I would think these thoughts often as the river flowed by. Although many people think a child of five couldn't have such thoughts, I did and I believe other children do as well. Unfortunately, it took many years before I found clarity in life and gained perspective on this strange spiritual experience. I can't put my finger on the exact reasons how and why this all took place. I just know that sometimes before life gets better, it can get worse. Much worse.

Hope Crushed

As a sixth-grader, a classmate invited me to join him for something called "Confirmation Class" at a church near my home. He explained it's where we learn more about his church and the Bible.

Because of our friendship, I agreed to go, excited that I might *really* get to know God.

Sadly, it was one of the most boring classes I ever attended! It continued for six long weeks; but each week I went excitedly hoping to get to know God. Never happened. At the end of these sessions the pastor went around the class asking each child if they wanted to join the church. Although everyone else nodded their affirmation, when he reached me I replied, "No."

"Why not"? He said with a puzzled look on his face.

"I don't know. But I am not joining".

Looking back, I believe my human spirit was excited but crushed by the humdrum nature of the presentation. So I turned my focus to football, wrestling, and girls as I entered my teenage years. I worked out incessantly and dreamed of becoming an athletic star. My dream came true my senior year in high school when I became a key player on our undefeated football team and captain of the wrestling squad.

One vivid memory from that football season took place during a pivotal game. Losing at half time, it appeared our undefeated season was in jeopardy. To make matters worse, I had sustained a serious ankle injury. Not knowing what else to do, I cried out to God: "Please let me go back into the game and score the winning touchdown..." then, "...Lord, I don't even need credit for the touchdown!"

That's exactly what happened! After I hobbled into the end zone, a reporter for the city's newspaper mistakenly credited our tailback with the winning touchdown. Although secretly I wished I hadn't said the last part of that prayer, it made God very real.

Another time He answered my plea for help on a college test, literally giving me a photographic memory during a final exam. WOW! It demonstrated to me His miraculous nature, although this kind of thing never happened again.

Still, He kept proving Himself real. In my early twenties, God kept me from serious injuries when the driver of the car I was riding in totaled his car. I should have died.

Then, at the age of twenty-six while hitchhiking through Ireland, He supernaturally directed me to a Catholic monastery. There I met a monk about my age who seemed to know God like a friend. He had a powerful impact on the search that would see me go through considerable struggle and conflict.

Ironically, I almost missed out on this experience in a rural area of Ireland. As I walked down the road hoping to catch another ride, huge, dark clouds rolled over my head. "*Maybe I better head back to town*," I thought. Then I said, "God, what should I do?"

Just then I looked toward the monastery. My eyes grew wide as the clouds parted, revealing a white cross made of clouds nestled in a circle of blue. I dove into the contents of my backpack to grab my camera, but by the time I could get ready to snap the picture, the image had vanished. I took this as a sign from God directing me to the monastery. Thankfully I went in the pouring rain, and I wound up staying there for a week talking to this monk a lot about God, Jesus, and the Holy Spirit.

Even that supernatural encounter with the monk didn't lead me directly to God. I continued searching desperately down dead ends. Growing up near that small, lifeless church, I was hungry for spiritual experiences, so one day I impulsively decided to give Zen Buddhism a try. I signed up to attend a seminar in New York City; afterwards I consistently meditated for forty minutes in the morning and another forty minutes in the evening. This had a calming effect, and at times, I could sense God's presence.

Chapter 2:

Seeking to Find God

Meditation alone couldn't turn aside the natural impulses or temptations of my youth. After college I got involved with psychedelic drugs like LSD and mescaline, and smoked massive amounts of marijuana. It may sound like some kind of lame excuse for partying, but deep down I did this in hopes of finding God-or at least escaping the meaninglessness of life. I was so hungry for the supernatural (which I had not seen in a church) that I plunged into this search with even greater passion. I even attended séances where spirits would come back from the dead and talk.

At that time I had no knowledge this was deceptive. My spiritual emptiness reflected my physical wandering. I hitchhiked across the country to California. I drifted and lived in different places. There I came under the influence of a woman from San Jose who was a key leader in the New Age Movement. The author of books on mystical topics, she told me I was gifted with psychic powers. She also trained me how to channel "ancient spirits," which I found quite exciting.

Like millions of others, I was hungry for the supernatural, and not knowing where to find it I looked in the wrong places. Later, through a tragic personal experience I realized just how deceived I had been.

A girl I was living with got pregnant and was weighing whether or not to have an abortion. Naturally, I turned to the "ancient spirit guide" for answers. He convinced both of us that it would be best to "free" the child from a hard life. This demon, disguised as 'ancient wisdom', went on to explain in flowery language that keeping the baby would be selfish. As a result, I took her to an abortion clinic. (I deeply regret this and still feel the pain of this error.)

Many have asked me why I tried to find God in a religion like Zen Buddhism – a religion that doesn't even believe in God. I know now that wasn't too smart, but in the midst of doing so many drugs I just couldn't see church as an avenue to God. The only ones I had ever been in seemed to have no spiritual life, no trace of the supernatural I craved.

It wasn't just alternative religions that drew my attention. For a while I lived on a commune in the Santa Cruz Mountains called "The Land." I had hoped to find deeper meaning in life by having sexual relations with a series of different women, but this just left me feeling emptier. Fortunately, I met a man there named Ralph, a cowboy who glowed with God's love. He would stop by to help us aimless hippies in practical ways, such as showing us how to care for our animals and raise organic crops. I was drawn to him because of his love and lack of judgment toward us. He would often offer words of personal encouragement.

The last time Ralph visited the commune he pointed at two of my friends, Suzanne and David, and me before saying, "You three will come to know the Lord, but J.R., you will go through some deep darkness first."

Painful Reality

Turns out that Ralph was a sage and what he predicted came true. I would continue in drugs, broken relationships, and later end up in jail in an Israeli prison for several weeks. I had crossed the border illegally. Had the police been able to find the drugs a friend and I ditched in the nick of time, my sentence would have been a lot longer. Many other dark things occurred during those years, causing me to despair of life itself. I felt like a boat adrift in the ocean with no purpose or destination. Life was so depressing any escape was welcome.

Along this troubled journey I suffered through a bad LSD trip that vividly revealed the emptiness of my personal life. It portrayed a lonely, painful future ahead of me. I was too drugged up to realize I needed to make adjustments to prevent that from happening. While still in California, I got so involved in "channeling" through my psychic mentor that it drove me deeper into despair. My life was a never-ending string of painful, broken relationships with women and lacked any sense of purpose. It seemed like everything was headed in a downward spiral.

At one of the lowest points in my life I received a letter from Suzanne and John Hunter, a couple I had known at the commune. More of Ralph's prophecy had come true. Suzanne and John said they had "found Jesus" while on a wandering trip through Asia, en route to India to find their guru. I wasn't convinced. Although their letter described their new found faith, it sounded pretty narrow minded to me. They wrote things like "Jesus is the only way to God," and told me how I needed to receive Jesus as my Lord and Savior or I would go to Hell. They said they were coming to visit me in California.

By then, I had married a girl I was living with, and we moved about forty-five miles south to Pacific Grove/ Monterrey, California. There I ran the local Buddhist meditation center. We lived upstairs while people would come twice daily to meditate in a large room downstairs. Even though Suzanne and John seemed a little fanatical about Jesus, I still looked forward to seeing them. Sure enough when they arrived, they didn't waste any time talking about Jesus. Although John did most of the talking, I noticed a new peace in Suzanne that I had not seen before. Still they came on so strong, I remember arguing a lot. This went on for three hours. Later, John told me he felt like he wasn't getting through and was so frustrated. He went into our bathroom, took authority over all the demonic resistance, and flushed the toilet! Thank God for crazy friends!

Well it worked! When he came out, there was a totally different atmosphere, and that evening I asked Jesus Christ to forgive my multitude of sin, to come into my life, and make me the person He wanted me to be! In fact, my prayer was something like this, "Jesus, I'm a mess; my life's a mess. If you can do anything with this screwed up person (me), please come into my life and good luck." My wife prayed to receive Jesus also. Now I didn't hear any voices from heaven or see any flashes of lightning. In fact I felt nothing. But strangely over the next few weeks my life began to change in subtle ways.

John gave me a prophecy that night saying "I would bear much fruit." I was puzzled not understanding Christian lingo. I thought maybe I would be growing fruit, perhaps in an orchard. John and Suzanne Hunter have been with Youth With A Mission (YWAM) ever since and presently run a school and orphanage in Namibia. I am deeply grateful to them, and they remain great friends.

They stayed with us that night and prayed with us to find a church home. The next day they drove back to L.A. where they were living. I remember I wasn't sure what to do. I told people who were coming to the zendo that now we pray instead of meditate. This was met with some curiosity but mostly anger and animosity.

We began to look for a church to attend. The first Sunday we went to a beautiful little church surrounded by redwoods, but it was pretty uninspiring. The next week after looking through the phone book, we went to a Christian Science church. Ironically, when we arrived, we realized they were meeting in a funeral parlor! This was very appropriate because I could tell, as a newborn Christian, that there was no life in that church!

The following week we traveled to Big Sur, about an hour away, and found a large group meeting at a Grange Hall. The music was lively; there were long haired Jesus freaks like us, which made us feel at home. Also, I could sense the presence of God there with us during worship. The services were very alive, and there seemed to be something – I didn't know what to call it then, but there was a presence which I had never experienced in a church. It was the Holy Spirit. The message was very practical and from the Bible. Then after service, members would have a potluck meal and discuss a multitude of basic things in the afternoon. Even though it was one hour away, we traveled down there every Sunday and began to grow in Christ. As one pastor put it: "A church alive is worth the drive!" We were introduced to a realm of spiritual areas: prophecy, tongues, spiritual warfare, healthy holiness (coming out of our sinful lifestyle), and Christian Community. Wow, what a difference it was making, but I still had a long way to go.

Chapter 3:

The Next Step

My life didn't seem aimless anymore. I was no longer full of despair, but I was wondering what God wanted me to do with my life. I was now 29 years old and although Jesus had come into my life, I still needed direction. We also had our first child which was a reality check. I prayed earnestly for God to direct my steps. I thought maybe He wanted me to be a Christian chiropractor. I had come to know a chiropractor in Pacific Grove who would adjust and pray for people. I had received some healing from some old athletic injuries, so this seemed perfect. I traveled to Portland, Oregon where I interviewed at Western States Chiropractic School. They told me they would accept me, so I bought two of the books intending to enroll in September.

Two weeks later a pastor invited me to a two day seminar. I asked him why he had invited me to meetings where everyone was a pastor but me. He smiled and said: "I thought you might enjoy it." I really did, and the second day I told him I think God wants me to be a pastor! Suddenly all kinds of people surrounded me, praying and prophesying over me.

At 29 I felt like I was too old to go to Bible School. I was warned against attending seminary because it was too liberal. I prayed to the Lord to direct me. When I was back visiting my family, I felt prompted to go over to Princeton Theological Seminary, which was about 25 minutes from my parent's house.

The campus was impressive, but I thought my prior grades in college would prohibit me from getting in. I wandered into the "Admissions Office" and the Admissions Director walked out and invited me in. After telling him my story, he said, "I believe you are to come to this school, and I am going to offer you a full scholarship." I guess he could tell I wasn't making much money and had a new baby. I said "That's very generous of you, but you haven't seen my grades from college." He said "I don't care about your grades!"

So the three of us traveled across the country, and I began my first year at Princeton Theological Seminary. Wow! What an adventure! Life at P.T.S. was hectic. Not only was I a full time seminary student and youth pastor; I also led a home group on Thursday nights and would minister with Reverend Richard Weir on Friday nights at his healing services. Needless to say I was more than busy, but I loved life and the excitement of my routine.

In the midst of all of this, I was given the painting company called "Painting by Seminary Students." This became a great source of income and a blessing. I hired one of my best friends, Bill Gaskill, who had also been a Zen Buddhist. He received Christ while on an LSD trip. His best friend died in his arms, after falling off a cliff, and this traumatic experience led to Bill's salvation. We naturally hit it off. It turned out he had been a professional painter. BINGO! The Holy Spirit was definitely in this one and had put us together. We were blessed financially, and Bill and I are still close friends after all of these years. (He pastors a church in New Jersey). Following the leading of the Holy Spirit can make life an exciting adventure!

Off to Seminary

I attended P.T.S. from September '75 to June '78. It was challenging, yet I believe it was God's plan for my life. I was exposed to liberal theology, but instead of weakening my faith, it strengthened it. I saw many flaws in this philosophy as I dove into God's Word. I prayed a lot while in seminary! I remember my first year Old Testament 101 class where a liberal professor explained it really wasn't the "Red Sea" but the "Reed Sea" that the Israelites came through from Egypt. He said the "Reed" Sea was only 4 to 5 inches deep. At the end of class he asked if anyone had questions. I said "I'm confused because that makes it a greater miracle. You mean Pharaoh's army drowned in only 4 to 5 inches of water?" The class laughed, but the professor was not amused.

I was fortunate to take most of my Biblical courses from Dr. Bruce Metzger, considered one of the foremost conservative scholars of the day. He had a strong personal relationship with Jesus and would pray at the beginning of every class. This would invite the presence of the Holy Spirit, and he would explain deep revelation from the scriptures in a clear way. I was also the youth pastor in a large Presbyterian church where Pastor Ernie Moritz was very open to the Holy Spirit. He would have me preach on Pentecost Sunday and encourage me not to hold back! My life was moving quickly and the Holy Spirit was playing a major role.

Then I was influenced by a man who knew the Holy Spirit and His power intimately. Pastor Richard Weir had come from England where he had received the left foot of fellowship from his denomination because he believed in the gifts of the Spirit and had a powerful healing ministry. He would hold services on Friday nights and fill Ernie's church beyond capacity. The worship ushered in God's presence, and he would preach God's Word with a wonderful British accent. Healing lines would form at the end of the service, and he would often be there praying for people until midnight. Richard approached me and asked me to help him pray for people. Before he would allow me to work with him, he insisted that I go through intensive deliverance. This was very helpful as I manifested the demonic and cried out for forgiveness in specific areas of sin while releasing forgiveness to those who had hurt me. One day I spent 10 hours with his deliverance team. I experienced great freedom and learned a lot about how the Holy Spirit sets us free from bad decisions, hang ups, and past traumatic pain.

The Moment of Reckoning

Pastor Ernie asked me to preach one day. It would be my first time ever preaching in a church. I told him I was more comfortable talking to youth in my role of youth pastor. I had come precariously close to failing public speaking at Wesleyan University, and this affected my confidence. My professor, Dr Markcraft had only passed me out of sympathy because he thought my brother had died in a car accident the week of my final speech. I never told him that it was a classmate, Chris Palamis' brother, not mine. The fact is, I was terrified to speak in front of a group of people, especially the size of Ernie's church with two services. He didn't know this of course, and insisted. After arguing with my senior pastor, I finally said yes. Anxiety gripped me for weeks as the Sunday approached.

Saturday night before I was to preach I was really nervous. I could not sleep, so I got up at midnight, 2:00 am, 4:00 am, and 6:00 am. I went outside and knelt by a tree each time recommitting my life to Jesus. I really felt that maybe I had made a terrible mistake pursuing pastoring. *Why didn't I become a chiropractor*? I thought. I felt like I was in my "Garden of Gethsemane," and I exclaimed "Not my will but Yours be done!" I cried out for the Holy Spirit's help in utter desperation!

The 40 minute ride to the church Sunday morning seemed like an eternity. At the 9:00 am service Pastor Ernie introduced me, and I stood up and walked to the pulpit. Fortunately, they had me wear a robe and people couldn't see my knees having fellowship with each other. I was terrified!

I preached everything I knew in 20 minutes. If you saw a video of my message, you would not have been impressed, but God helped me, and I got through it. I had asked Pastor Ernie if I could give people a chance to receive Christ. (It was not the practice in this Presbyterian Church). He had graciously said yes. As I gave the opportunity, I almost fell out of the pulpit as three hands went up to receive Christ. I led everyone in the "Sinner's Prayer" and was so excited that I could hardly wait for the 11 o'clock service. In that service two people received Christ. I knew that the Holy Spirit was with me, and it didn't depend on my great oratorical ability. It relaxed me a little, and I almost looked forward to my next opportunity to speak two months later. But I was still pretty uptight about it. I was learning to depend on the Holy Spirit with fear and trembling!

I am convinced that God is looking for availability more than ability. What God appoints, He will anoint! "*It is not by might, nor by power but by my Spirit, says the Lord*." (Zech. 4:6)

The BIG Decision

Spring had sprung in Princeton with its budding plants, beautiful flowers and serenading birds. All of creation seemed to be coming alive as winter faded away, but a gnawing anxiety began to arise inside of me. I knew that soon I must leave the familiar nest and routine of P.T.S. and launch out into the church world. My life at seminary had been full. We arrived there with our son, Mike, who was now 3 years old. While in seminary our second child, Anna, was born. Being at their births was definitely one of the highlights of my life, and seeing birth happen made me realize at a deeper level that God is so real. How else could life come forth? I loved my children so much, but it was more mouths to feed. My wife poured herself into the kids, so I needed to bring home the bread!

I graduated in June of 1978, and the Holy Spirit led me to a small church in Grand Lake, Colorado. I went there not knowing how to be a pastor and feeling very insecure. So although deeply in love with Jesus, I so depended on the Holy Spirit. I had seen the Holy Spirit move powerfully under Richard Weir's ministry, so I was eager to hopefully see Him move in Colorado too, but things would not go smoothly. Little did I know that several from the little church of about 40 people in Grand Lake would not appreciate my guitar led worship and praying for the sick.

After an extremely difficult time, a church split, fostered by the denomination, plus other struggles, we experienced a "revival." That little church saw people come into a relationship with God, healed physically and emotionally, and delivered from past trauma. It was so exciting and continued for many months. The church grew to 300 plus people attending on Sundays in a town with a population of only 500, but much more exciting than numbers was the tangible presence of the Holy Spirit. God had shown Himself faithful! Seventeen people went into missions work or pastoring from there, and we planted a sister church in Winter Park, Colorado. Life in the Spirit was good!

I am now the lead pastor of a church with wonderful people hungry for the Spirit. It is called "The Rock", and it is in Castle Rock, Colorado (www.therock.org). When I came to the church, we struggled with maybe about 70 people and $50,000 in debt while meeting in a rundown warehouse. We went through many trials, but we saw so many people transformed by the power of the Holy Spirit. The church has now grown to around 1200 to 1400 in attendance on Sundays. Life in the Spirit is exciting, fun, yet challenging.

Hopefully, this background of my life will help you understand the principles I will be sharing on how to live "Life in the Spirit." Also, let me make it very clear, it is not so much how many people are in a church, but how many lives are being transformed! Jesus changed the world with only 12 individuals and one of those turned out to be a jerk.

The Holy Spirit has played a vital role in my life teaching me why and how He is so powerful. When I went from Zen Buddhism and staring at a wall, to suddenly having communication with the living God, it was so exciting. God was real! He was alive. Instead of just clearing my mind, it was like going from two dimensions to three dimensions. I thought, *Wow, now, I know God loves me; I know He's with me*. But the Holy Spirit was the part of the Godhead that really changed my life. He was the one who communicated with me, led me, convicted me, empowered me and comforted me in hard times. He will do the same for you. Let's talk about it.

Section 2

AN IMPORTANT ROLE OF THE HOLY SPIRIT

"O Holy Spirit, descend plentifully into my heart. Enlighten the dark corners of this neglected dwelling and scatter there thy cheerful beams."
- Augustine

In the American church the Holy Spirit is often misunderstood or ignored. This is as ironic as it is sad, because He – the Holy Spirit- is a vital part of the Godhead. In fact He is the one who has the most direct contact with us on earth and is our constant point of connection with the triune God. He is the one who changes us from the inside out. One of the roles of the Holy Spirit is to help us by lovingly bringing correction (conviction). We all need this kind of help because we are human!

Chapter 4:

Addicted and Changed

After discovering this incredible relationship with Father, Son and Holy Spirit, I was overwhelmed by His love for me. I had felt that my sordid past made me unlovable, but I now felt deeply loved. My life style still really needed help. There were well meaning Christians who were attempting to help me change, but their primary methods were condemnation and shame. That did not work very well for me. Have you noticed that religion doesn't really change people, but a loving relationship with the Holy Spirit does?

Don't you see how wonderfully kind, tolerant, and patient God is with you? Does this mean nothing to you? Can't you see that his kindness is intended to turn you from your sin?
(Romans 2:4 NLT)

After becoming a believer, I was still deeply addicted to marijuana. I know some say that is not possible, but it was true for me. I couldn't play my guitar, go to a social gathering, attend a movie, or get to sleep without smoking weed. I grew my own and played my guitar and meditated under its influence almost every day. I was deeply connected.

A well meaning Christian named Barbara would say to me, "You can't smoke marijuana now because you are a Christian." I would retaliate by telling her to show me in scripture where it says "Thou shalt not smoke marijuana." She was frustrated with me. If she had known scripture better, she might have pointed me to Ephesians 5:18 which says: "Don't be drunk with wine, because that will ruin your life. Instead, be filled with the Holy Spirit..." She could have pointed out that being stoned and drunk was something God said could hurt our lives while being filled with the Holy Spirit was a much better and safer high. That would have made me think twice.

So rejecting Barbara's condemning approach, I prayed a simple, honest prayer. "Lord, you are the most important person in my life, if this weed is coming between You and me, I don't want it. But You will have to show me." See I knew if I stopped smoking marijuana because Barbara said I should, I might do fine for a week or two. But then I would roll a huge joint and blow my mind. I knew me, but I wanted God's best.

It's funny how God answered that prayer. About three weeks later, Harvey Berman, a friend I had been praying for, stopped by my house. He pulled out some very strong weed, and we smoked it. Then he asked me a question I will never forget. He said "Tell me about this Jesus that you are into."

What an incredible opportunity! I tried my best in a stoned stupor and stammered,. "Well Jesus is really far out..." "He's the ultimate trip..." I struggled for the words and my mind seemed uncooperative. He looked like a calf looking at a new gate as I tried to explain the most important person in my life. He left unmoved, and I went back into my bedroom and lay down on the bed.

As I lay there, I felt this heaviness come over me, not condemning, but more like a deep sadness. I didn't know what it was but later realized it was the "conviction" of the Holy Spirit who was trying to help me. I also felt sad I couldn't convey my heart to my friend Harvey. Then a strange thing happened. The Lord impressed on me that marijuana didn't make me high as I supposed. Instead it was like pouring a thick coating of molasses over my head, my brain, my eyes, my mouth and my entire body. I thought *Wow, I don't need this stuff.* I asked the Lord to forgive me. I got up off the bed and grabbed this huge glass container I had hidden behind clothes in my closet. I went to that same toilet John Hunter had flushed the "demons" down several weeks earlier, and flushed the entire contents down the toilet. It took about 10 flushes. Then I put the glass container down and raised my hands to heaven: "Thank you, Jesus."

The scripture says when you know the truth it sets you free, and I was free indeed.

Ironically, the state of Colorado was the first state to legalize marijuana (2013). I'm not against it for medicinal purposes; my own mother was helped by this herb while she was dying of cancer. But I believe marijuana can be abused just like prescription drugs, alcohol, or any substance that can alter your mind and emotions. Listen, I am not a legalist, and I don't believe Jesus was a legalist. I will be honest; I often enjoy a glass of wine with my dinner. After all His first miracle was when He changed the water to wine! But for me personally, marijuana was destructive. It is the only time in my life since junior high when I was not exercising regularly and was out of shape. My use of marijuana took my drive and energy. So for me it was a detrimental escape from reality. The Holy Spirit set me so free I have never had the slightest desire to smoke it again.

The Holy Spirit brings conviction (clarity) into our lives to help us not to hurt us. "And when He (the Holy Spirit) comes, He will convict and convince the world and bring demonstration to it about sin and about righteousness (uprightness of heart and right standing with God) and about judgment" to it about sin and about righteousness (uprightness of heart and right standing with God) and about judgement" (John 16:8 AMP).

The Greek word "elencho," translated convict and convince, can mean to bring to light, to change the way a person sees things. That is how it is used here. Notice it refers to "righteousness." So the Holy Spirit also convinces us of our right standing with God even when we make a mistake. Maybe an even better word than convict (which sounds condemning) would be "convince" or "clearly reveal." This is what the Holy Spirit does for us.

A Battle with Lust

About twelve years ago I was struggling with lust for a woman I was helping. She had been a former beauty queen and was still very attractive. She came to me complaining about her abusive husband. My heart hurt for her, and she began calling me frequently, coming to my office where I would counsel her. I really enjoyed these sessions. We were both becoming emotionally involved. I began to fantasize about her in sexual ways. I was both stimulated and scared by my feelings. I was happily married with two great kids. Nothing sexual had happened yet, but I could see where this was heading. DANGER!

The Holy Spirit was trying to get through to me, but I was enjoying her attention too much. Then the turning point came. My wife, Yvonne, and I were out to lunch at the local Village Inn with our closest friends. They were pastors of a church in Colorado Springs, and we had vacationed together and spent time sharing honestly about life. I felt the Holy Spirit strongly impress upon me to share the struggle I was going through right then. But I thought to myself: *No, I can't bring this up now because Yvonne doesn't even know about it, and after all it is just fantasy; nothing has happened.* But it got stronger and stronger that I should bring this out in the open with Yvonne and our best friends.

So I blurted out, "Friends I really need prayer about something."

I shared the whole struggle and watched Yvonne's reaction. She was calm and just listened. My friend, Dan, shared how he was going through a similar battle with lust and would we pray for him as well. I have no idea what we ate for lunch that day, but I do know a heavy weight of condemnation and sexual temptation was lifted off my shoulders. It was finally brought to the light. We all four hugged as we said goodbye after the meal.

Thanks to the Holy Spirit, I had dodged a major bullet.

If we say that we have fellowship with Him, and walk in darkness, we lie and do not practice the truth. But if we walk in the light as He is in the light, we have fellowship with one another, and the blood of Jesus Christ His Son cleanses us from all sin. If we say that we have no sin, we deceive ourselves, and the truth is not in us. If we confess our sins, He is faithful and just to forgive us our sins and to cleanse us from all unrighteousness.

(1 John 1:6-9)

I was no longer walking in darkness, thank God! The next day this lady called to ask if we could meet. I said I was really sorry, but I no longer felt I could counsel her. I offered the services of my wife which she politely declined and that ended it. Even when I would see her in church, I no longer had lust, I was fine! Thank you Holy Spirit!

Confess your sins to each other and pray for each other so that you may be healed (delivered). The earnest prayer of a righteous person has great power and produces wonderful results.
(James 5:16 NLT)

The word used for "sins" in this passage is not the usual Greek word "hamartia" which means to "miss the mark" and refers to act of sin. But the Greek word here is "paraptoma" which literally means "to take a false step." Thus, if we confess that "false step" and bring it to the light before it becomes blatant sin, we can be rescued. This Greek word means delivered as well as healed. When I was in that situation I needed deliverance not healing. The Amplified Bible explains this in depth.

Therefore, confess your sins to one another [your false steps, your offenses], and pray for one another, that you may be healed and restored.
(James 5:16 AMP)

Section 3

The Empowering of The Holy Spirit

"Since the days of Pentecost, has the whole church ever put aside every other work and waited upon Him for ten days that the Spirit's power might be manifested? We give too much attention to method, machinery, and resources, and too little to the source of power."
– Hudson Taylor

Talking about the "Empowering of the Holy Spirit" can be a controversial topic. In this and succeeding sections you may read things that are different from what you believe or what you've been taught. I ask you to keep an open mind, pray and check it out by the Word. Always bring things back to God's Word and allow it to guide you. It will be a "lamp for your feet and a light for your path."

Chapter 5:

How Can We Make a Difference in This World?

The Holy Spirit is definitely the key. In the book of Acts we see the powerful effect the Holy Spirit had on a non-Christian world.

Then the churches throughout all Judea, Galilee, and Samaria had peace and were edified. And walking in the fear of the Lord and in the comfort of the Holy Spirit, they were multiplied.
(Acts 9:31)

Notice that Christians in the early church were being persecuted, yet because they were in this awe (fear) of God and the comfort of the Holy Spirit that the churches were multiplied in the midst of all their pain. This was impacting the culture of the day powerfully.

We are seeing that happening now in places like China, Pakistan, India, African countries, Latin American countries and throughout the Middle East. God is moving in the Muslim, Buddhist and Hindu world despite heavy persecution. We are seeing the Holy Spirit making a difference just like in the Book of Acts. When I was in Pakistan just recently my heart went out to the people there. To be a Christian in Pakistan is very difficult. I had an opportunity to minister to hundreds of persecuted church leaders and was moved to tears by their courage and willingness to suffer for the cause of Christ. Jesus' heart goes out to those people. He died on a cross to bring life and hope, and they want others to know that.

If you are reproached for the name of Christ, blessed are you, for the Spirit of glory and of God rests upon you. On their part He is blasphemed, but on your part He is glorified.
(1 Peter 4:14)

In the United States, it is amazing that Christianity is the only religion that people seem to get uptight about. In many schools you can talk about Islam; you can talk about Buddhism and Hinduism, but if you talk about Christianity you are probably going to get censored. There is an enemy, and he doesn't like the Gospel!

So how do we receive the strength and the empowering needed to fulfill our destiny? It is simple: *Not by might nor by power, but by my Spirit, says the Lord of Hosts*. (Zechariah 4:6). Sometimes we think it is by our own power or abilities, that we can accomplish things by our own personality. True, we can help people, but we can help them so much more effectively, by the power and help of the Holy Spirit. This is what changes people's lives!

We can accomplish a lot through programs and our own abilities, but the Holy Spirit is essential to producing what really matters and lasts over the long haul. I have pastored for many years and found this to be so true. We have a fairly large church, but it is not the size that is important. It is the power of the Holy Spirit changing and transforming lives that matters most.

We sing a song that says: *"break our heart for what breaks yours."* We want the Holy Spirit to not only change us from the inside out to become more like Jesus, but also to really break us of self and our agenda, and bring us into the place of His agenda. That is how impartation comes. If you think you have all you need to accomplish all God wants you to do, then I say you are thinking too small and that your vision is probably yours, not God's. He calls us to do things that are beyond our ability. And He does that so we will have to be dependent on the Holy Spirit. If we could do it in our own power, we could get big heads and say, "Look what I've done for you, God." That doesn't impress Him. God wants to be a part of our lives and He loves to produce some great things through us. He wants to partner with us. But, as long as we are doing it in our own power, He allows us to do it on our own and flounder around in our own strength. We must be open and dependent on Him!

If Jesus Needed to Be Empowered by the Holy Spirit, What About Us?

Jesus could not begin His ministry until He was baptized (empowered) by the Holy Spirit. The only thing mentioned about Jesus before this event is that He confounded some of the Scribes and Pharisees in the Temple at twelve years old. There is no mention of any great things He did. There were no miracles, healings, deliverances, etc. ...nothing miraculous occurred until after He was baptized by the Holy Spirit.

"When all the people were being baptized, Jesus was baptized, too. And, as he was praying, heaven was opened and the Holy Spirit

descended on him in bodily form like a dove." (Luke 3:21-23a NIV) Now some movies portray a literal dove descending from Heaven but it was not a dove. The Holy Spirit descended <u>*like*</u> a dove. How does a dove descend? Very gently. Not like an eagle swooping down but slowly and deliberately. *"And a voice came from heaven: You are my Son whom I love; with you I am well pleased."* Notice we have <u>Jesus</u> the Son being baptized, the <u>Spirit</u> descending upon Him, and then we have the <u>Father</u> speaking out of Heaven affirming His Son. The Trinity is at work here.

I believe if we could hear the Father, we would often hear Him say that He is well pleased with us, His sons and daughters. If you can experience the pleasure of the Father and the power of the Holy Spirit and the love of the Son, it will change the way you view and relate to God. Jesus didn't just start healing people; He first goes into the wilderness and battles Satan for 40 days. Then He comes out in miraculous power. It is only at that time that the healings and miracles begin!

So we should not strive, but be available to be used in powerful ways by God. *Now Jesus Himself was about 30 years old when He began His ministry.* This fact encouraged me because I did not get saved until I was 28 ½ years old. I felt like I was so far behind, and getting such a late start when I entered seminary at age 30. That's why when I came to the Lord I wanted everything he could give me. I realized that I was not particularly gifted, and that I would need all the help I could get. One of the churches I first attended said we shouldn't talk about the Holy Spirit, because we didn't understand Him and the gifts had passed away centuries ago. That church was very dead! I didn't stay there long.

Jesus, full of the Holy Spirit, (this is just after he got baptized) *left the Jordan and was led by the Spirit into the wilderness...* (Luke

4:1-2a NIV) You may be asking if it really was the Holy Spirit that led Jesus into the wilderness, since it seems that is something Satan would do. No, it was the Holy Spirit!

It is important to realize that sometimes the Holy Spirit leads us into places that are difficult. We are not on this earth to be comfortable. If you thought receiving Jesus would make your life comfortable and easy, I am here to tell you that is not true. You will be comfortable in Heaven, but while you are here, you are here to make a difference and often that means discomfort. *Jesus was led into a place "where for forty days he was tempted by the devil.* The Holy Spirit led him into the battle. Often when you are doing what God has called you to do, the enemy will come against you. We may question if we are in God's will because of difficulty. Yes, struggles come when you are definitely in God's will. The enemy just happens to hate our guts.

Power through Trials

I almost died at birth and had to be extracted with forceps. But, Jesus wanted me alive. I died at 4 ½ but Jesus brought me back to life. One of my brothers told me that every time an ambulance would come to our house to take me, he would panic because he thought I was going to die. The devil tried to kill me several times. Just remember the greater One is on the inside of us no matter what the enemy tries to do. Scripture tells us "greater is He who is in me than He who is in the world." (I John 4:4) So who is in you? The Holy Spirit! He is in you making you stronger beyond your natural weakness. In the battles we become stronger in Him!

Many years ago a stranger tried to kill me during a church service. It was on a Sunday night, and I was pastoring up in the mountains. I had only been in the church about a year. This guy came at me and attacked me. I will finish the story later when I cover the gifts of the Spirit and how Jesus saved my life through the gift of faith and the Holy Spirit intervening (so read on)! When I travel to Pakistan each year with Leif Hetland our lives are often threatened, but machine gun body guards and the Holy Spirit have kept us safe over the years!

Jesus was in the wilderness for 40 days and 40 nights and He used the Word of God. Satan quoted Psalm 91. The devil said*; Cast yourself off this high place, for your angels have charge over You.* Satan tempted Jesus with suicide but Jesus retaliated with the Word: "You shall not tempt the Lord your God". When Jesus told Satan to get behind Him, He had won the battle. Notice this battle did not occur until after Jesus was baptized in the Holy Spirit. Now here is the cool part. That battle changed Jesus; He became much stronger in the Spirit. I can prove it: "*Jesus returned to Galilee in the <u>power</u> of the Spirit, and news about Him spread through the whole countryside.*" (Luke 4:14 NIV, emphasis mine).

For you to really operate in power, you are going to have to go through some trials, temptations, battles, and struggles. How do you develop muscles? Is it by sitting on the couch watching TV and eating bonbons? No, you have to do resistance training. It takes resistance from weights and sweat to build physical strength. How do you build stronger lungs? It is when you go out and run and push through the desire to give up

In life, we have resistance. We have an enemy. In John 10:10 it says that the thief (Satan) comes to "steal, kill and destroy." The enemy hates anyone that is a believer in Jesus and is doing something for the Kingdom of God. Before I was a follower, I would fall into temptation. I thought I was having fun, but honestly, my life was a mess. When I became a believer, I saw temptation and sin was not fun, but it was the enemy's tactics. The good news is that when Jesus said that the thief came to steal, kill and destroy. He added: "but I came that you may have life and have it more abundantly" (John 10:10).

No matter how bad the trials and the battles, you will come through and be stronger if you will trust the Holy Spirit. That's how we grow. When a trial comes, don't be upset, in fact, rejoice! Realize that God is going to strengthen you, and you are going to come out of the trial with more power and wisdom. In every struggle I have come through, I have realized something: trials give you more of a heart for people, especially those going through similar battles. I have a heart for those people because I have been through it. Because I understand the pain, I can better help them.

I was a single parent for a while; I know the struggles they go through, because I was one. Through all my trials God has made me stronger, and I've learned from them. I am a better person and pastor today because I endured these trials. Early in my walk when a couple in my church was going through a divorce, I would have a pat answer and give them a scripture. After I went through my own divorce, I felt their pain and could pray and minister to them with empathy. My counsel to them came from the Holy Spirit and from a heart of caring.

Recently, a couple who are close friends hit a major problem in their marriage. The wife felt her husband was having an affair which the husband denied. She found possible evidence, and things looked bleak as they separated. I found myself praying at different times of the day for them. The Lord would wake me up in the middle of the night praying and travailing in the Spirit. Also the Holy Spirit gave my wife and me wise counsel at this time with words of knowledge and wisdom.

I encouraged the husband to get into counseling immediately. My wife and I were able to reach out to his wife as well. We encouraged them not to give up. We gave them very strong advice, which, the spirit had revealed to us. They got into counseling immediately, and began to rebuild the broken trust brick by brick. It has taken time, and we have continued to pray. Miraculously, we saw God put this marriage back together and make it stronger than ever before. Prayer and the Holy Spirit are powerful agents of hope and change. No matter how bad things may look, remember He is the God of the impossible! He will use you to bring hope and healing.

Blessed be the God and Father of our Lord Jesus Christ, the Father of mercies and God of all comfort, who comforts us in all our tribulation, that we may be able to comfort those who are in any trouble, with the comfort with which we ourselves are comforted by God.
2 Corinthians 1:3-4

Empowered to Heal

Earlier I mentioned how Richard Weir had a very powerful healing ministry in Great Britain. He went through terrible persecution and rejection from his denomination. But he persevered, and said when he came to the U.S. the anointing increased considerably because of those trials.

Sometimes we not only have to persevere in trials but overcome our own insecurities for the Holy Spirit to operate through us. When Richard asked me to help him with his Friday night healing services, he asked me to pray for people along with him because the healing lines had gotten so long. I hadn't been a Christian that long, and I was still a student in seminary. When Richard would pray he had this great British accent and his hands would shake under the anointing. Many were healed and compared to him I felt extremely inadequate.

The first night I was to help, I was sitting up on the stage when the line began forming. I was already feeling apologetic for the ones that would be having me pray for them. I wanted to say, "Sorry, maybe next Friday you won't be so unlucky, and you will get Richard to pray for you."

That first night I was tempted to run down the aisle, get in my car, drive home and not pray for anybody. I felt so small, but the Holy Spirit came to my aid, thank God. He prompted me asking, "Who is the Healer and what did I ask you to do?"

At that point, I didn't even know that it was God's will to heal. I just thought it was something He does when He feels like it. I didn't know much, but I knew God was called "Jehovah Rapha", the Healer. I also knew that scripture at the end of the book of Mark which says, "And they will lay hands on the sick and they will recover." So I responded: "I will lay hands on the sick."

He then impressed on me: "Yes, and leave the recovery to me!"

Then the Holy Spirit showed me this rusty pair of battery cables. You might wonder why they were rusty. I have my own sense of what it meant. None of us are perfect conductors for him to flow through so He has to use "rusty" vessels. Let's imagine you are driving and somebody's car battery is dead on the side of the road. You pull up, and you go into your trunk and pull out this rusty, dirty pair of battery cables. Then you hook it up to your good battery. All of a sudden, their car starts. They don't remark "Those are such a cool pair of rusty battery cables you have!" See the Holy Spirit will help us in our inadequacy and ignorance if we look to Him. I saw many people healed just because I was willing... and was more surprised than they were!

I think a lot of people are afraid of praying for healing for the sick because they feel responsible for the results. What if they pray for someone and they don't get healed? They are afraid the person will be upset with God, and upset with them. They fear embarrassment. I was really set free that night, because I realized I am not the Healer. I realized I am like those battery cables. I am still "rusty," by the way. The bottom line is that it is His power. He is the one that flows through us when we lay hands on the sick- even when we are not perfect conductors. I have seen so many miracles and healings over the years! Every miracle and healing is performed by Him, but I got to be an important part. That is fun!

Chapter 6:

Do People See Jesus In You?

Often it is down in the trenches where we learn the most. The Holy Spirit is a great teacher- especially when the chips are down. Jesus walked with His disciples for 3 1/2 years. You think they would have had enough training because that's better than any seminary, Bible school or YWAM training. But even after all that personal time with the Master, they still had to learn from the Holy Spirit in the school of "Hard Knocks"! The book of Acts makes this clear.

Jesus knew they would need supernatural help so just before He died He said to them, "And now I will send the Holy Spirit, just as my Father promised. But stay here in the city until the Holy Spirit comes and fills you with power from Heaven" (Luke 24:49 NLT). In other words, those disciples, even though they spent more than 3 years with Jesus- still were not ready for Him to turn over the ministry to them until they received power from on high. Think about that. Now, if that is true about the disciples who walked with Jesus personally, how much more true is it for us?

The last words Jesus spoke before he ascended into heaven were: "But you will receive power when the Holy Spirit comes on you; and you will be My witnesses in Jerusalem, and in all Judea and Samaria, and to the ends of the earth." (Acts 1:8 NIV) The word here for power in the original language (Greek) is "dunamis." It is where we get the English word for "dynamite" or "dynamic." When it says you will receive power when the Holy Spirit comes on you, and you will be my witnesses, it doesn't mean you can witness better. The word "witness" here is the word "marturion" (in the Greek), and it is where we get the English word "martyr." The word in pure form meant that people would see the reality of Jesus in the believer. It took on the meaning that someone would die for Jesus.

In the early church, Christians would be fed to the lions and the spectators in the coliseum would see the peace and joy on their faces as the lions killed them. These Christians would be praising God because they knew in a few seconds they were going to be with Him! As the people in the stands saw this, many were so blown away that they would give their lives to Christ. "Martyr" became the word for someone who died for Christ, yet that was not the original meaning of the word.

If people are going to see Jesus in you, it is because of the power of the Holy Spirit working in and through you and His love in your heart. It's not going to be because you are nice looking, pretty or extremely talented. It will be because the Holy Spirit is operating in you that people will experience Jesus. But you must be willing to take risks and it must be done through a motivation of His love or it is pointless. In 2 Corinthians 5:14 Paul writes "For the love of Christ compels (motivates) us..." This love is powerful.

Remember I mentioned how in my mid 20s I lived in this commune called "The Land" in California where cowboy Ralph, would come visit us often. He would love us unconditionally and not judge us even though there were a lot of things that could have disgusted him. He would operate in the gifts of the Spirit giving us prophecies, encouragement, and pray for our healing and for our animals to be healed. I loved it. It was like he was reading our mail, in a good way. One day he brought his wife which was a big mistake. She was offended deeply and extremely judgmental. What a bummer. He said he would never be able to come back again. He said he was sorry, but his wife didn't understand us, and he loved his wife too much to offend her. "She feels that you don't wear enough clothing, your hair is too long, and you don't bathe enough, but I love you all so much." These were his parting words. He hugged us all and left. This guy had such an impact on my life. I know he planted seeds that later helped bring me to Jesus!

When I did finally receive Christ, I so wanted to see Ralph again, but I couldn't find him. Since he was a lot older, our reunion will have to wait until Heaven. I can't wait to hug him! Wow, did I see Jesus in Ralph! I hope people see Jesus in us!

Two "Lost" Hitchhikers

An amazing, encouraging event happened while I was pastoring in Grand Lake, Colorado. I was traveling to Kremmling, Colorado, about an hour away. I saw a couple standing along the road just outside of Grand Lake and felt the Holy Spirit nudge me to pick them up. Their names were Eric and Candy and they began to tell me they were headed to Kremmling and deeply appreciated the ride. They were young and definitely looked like "hippies" from their dress and hair.

As we chatted they said they were part of the group called "The Way!" I immediately felt a burden for them being caught up in this weird cult. I prayed and the Holy Spirit told me to talk to them about Jesus. 'The Way' was a cult run by Victor Paul Wierwille. They considered themselves Christians but had some very strange beliefs and few were saved. As I talked about Jesus, they responded, and were not defensive. I shared my testimony and asked if they needed help of any kind. I felt great compassion for them. They mentioned they were really out of money. I reached in my wallet and gave them the $23 I had. I mentioned some other things and asked them if Jesus was "really their Lord." I dropped them off in Kremmling thinking, *I will never see them again*.

Several years later, I was leading worship at an ecumenical conference in Vail, Colorado. We had assembled a worship team from the church I had just started attending in Greeley. I did not know the people on the team. The second day I was talking with the lead guitarist and simultaneously we realized we had met in the past. It was Eric, and his wife Candy was with him! In amazement we hugged each other, as they said my kindness and questions about Jesus being their Lord haunted them. They finally left "The Way", and became authentic followers of Jesus. They had moved to Greeley and just recently joined the worship team.

Wow, is God great! You never know when you reach out to someone by the leading of the Spirit in the love of Jesus, what kind of an impact it may have down the road!

Billy Graham's Baptism by the Holy Spirit

Someone who has demonstrated Jesus Christ to many over the years is Billy Graham. He probably has led more people to Christ than just about anyone who has ever lived. He has had a tremendous anointing for souls. Billy did not consider himself "Pentecostal" or "Charismatic," yet he was definitely baptized in the Holy Spirit. After being saved he spoke in private about how the "baptism" changed the course of his life and ministry. But let's hear about Billy's experience from a book entitled *The Leadership Secrets of Billy Graham*.

> Billy's soul was indeed ablaze. Unsophisticated, he was painfully aware of his limitations but he was full of passion to fulfill what he believed that God was calling him to: spreading the Gospel, "the Good News," as a message of liberation and love.
>
> Yet as he focused and energetically began preaching and receiving ever more invitations to speak, he sensed increasingly that his eloquence could not persuade or transform. His deepening humility was anchored in fact. He knew he was not an outstanding speaker and that his personal charisma was not enough to fulfill the great call he felt weighing upon him. He had entered a life of helplessness-helpless to do this work that was far greater than his capacities.
>
> As he found some success as an evangelist, he continually sought a greater connection and empowerment. During a mission to the British Isles, he met a young Welsh evangelist named Stephen Olford, who had the spiritual qualities Billy longed for. "He had a dynamic…exhilaration about him I wanted to capture." After hearing Olford preach on being filled with the Holy Spirit, Billy approached him and said, "You've spoken of something that I don't have. I want the fullness of the Holy Spirit in my life too."

Olford agreed to set aside two days when Billy was scheduled to speak at Pontypridd, just eleven miles from the home of Olford's parents. The two would talk and pray during the day, pausing long enough for Billy to preach at night.

"This is serious business," Billy told him. "I have to learn what this is that the Lord has been teaching you."

In the small stone hotel, Olford led Billy step by step through the Bible verses on the Spirit's power, which had produced Olford's profound spiritual renewal a few months earlier. The effects of the mentoring, however, were not evident in that evening's service

"Quite frankly," said Olford later, "his preaching was very ordinary. Neither his homiletics nor his theology nor his particular approach to Welsh people made much of an impact. The Welsh are masters of preaching, and they expect hard, long sermons with a couple of hours of solid exposition. Billy was giving brief little messages. They listened, but it wasn't their kind of preaching." The crowd was small, passive, and to Billy's invitation, unresponsive.

The next day Olford continued the instruction, telling Billy that he "must be broken" like the apostle Paul, letting God turn him inside out.

"I gave him my testimony of how God completely turned my life inside out-an experience of the Holy Spirit in his fullness and anointing," said Olford. "As I talked, and I can see him now, those marvelous eyes glistened with tears, and he said, 'Stephen, I see it. That's what I want. That's what I need in my life.'" Olford suggested they "pray this through," and both men knelt on the floor.

"I can still hear Billy pouring out his heart in a prayer of total dedication to the Lord," said Olford. "Finally, he said, 'My heart is so flooded with the Holy Spirit!' and we went from praying to praising. We were laughing and praising God, and Billy was walking back and forth across the room, crying out, 'I have it! I'm filled. This is a turning point in my life.' And he was a new man."

As Billy recalls the experience years later, "I was beginning to understand that Jesus himself was our victory, through the Holy Spirit's power."

That night, when Billy preached, "for reasons known to God alone, the place which was only moderately filled the night before was packed to the doors," said Olford. "As Billy rose to speak, he was a man absolutely anointed."

Members of the audience came forward to pray even before Billy gave an invitation. At the end of the sermon, practically the entire crowd rushed forward.

> "My own heart was so moved by Billy's authority and strength that I could hardly drive home," Olford remembers. "When I came in the door, my father looked at my face and said, "What on earth happened?" I sat down at the kitchen table and said, "Dad, something has happened to Billy Graham. The world is going to hear from this man.'[1]

We All Need Empowering

Sometimes the empowering of the Holy Spirit is dramatic, but other times it is subtle. In my own case it was a very subtle but powerful experience of His empowering. Don't put the Holy Spirit in a box. Let him empower you how He wants to. Just remember "Seek and you will find!" (Matt. 7:7)

God is looking for people who will change the world! That means in all realms of society He needs people to rise up and be filled with the Spirit to change our culture. That means people are needed in education, in the arts, in media, in business, in science and technology, and in the entertainment field, not just in the church world. Also, He makes us better people: husbands, wives, singles, parents, etc… We need Christians empowered by the Holy Spirit to change the world. That's why we are here!

Misconceptions About the Empowering

The Empowering is a One Time Filling

There are many misconceptions about the Holy Spirit's empowering. Let's look at some.

People who believe the Holy Spirit fills us once will often say, "This is how it happened with me; this is how it has to happen with you." But, God wants us filled on a continual basis. It is not just a onetime event where you pull up to the Holy Spirit gas pump, He fills you to overflowing, and He says "now drive carefully. Hopefully you will have enough power to get you through your journey. I will come back one day to get you. But, be careful because if your tank runs down, you are out of luck."

That is fortunately not true; the Holy Spirit continually fills us. He fills us in worship; He fills us in the Word and fellowship with others. Whenever we pray in the Spirit, He uses that opportunity to fill us too. At times when we are desperate, He comes. There are so many ways He continuously fills us; don't put the Holy Spirit in a box. Let Him do it the way He does it but make sure you cooperate with Him.

Let's look at scripture. "And do not get drunk with wine for that is debauchery; but ever be filled and stimulated with the Holy Spirit." (Ephesians 5:18 AMP) Most translations say "be filled with the Holy Spirit" but the original Greek translation is in the present progressive tense. If translated literally, it would say "be being filled on a regular basis." We need to be continually filled. We leak and get weary. But He is more than willing to fill us if we will just cry out to Him and go to Him in that place of brokenness and desperation. If we just cry out to Him, He will come and answer our plea.

> So I say to you: *"Ask and it will be given to you; seek and you will find; knock and the door will be opened to you. For everyone who asks receives; the one who seeks finds; and to the one who knocks, the door will be opened. Which of you fathers, if your son asks for a fish, will give him a snake instead? Or if he asks for*

an egg, will give him a scorpion? If you then, though you are evil, know how to give good gifts to your children, how much more will your Father in heaven give the Holy Spirit to those who ask Him!"

- Luke 11:9-13

Being filled with His Spirit gives us perseverance to not give up. When I was with Richard Weir, praying for those people coming forward and needing healing so badly, I was in a desperate place. Also, I felt deeply troubled because neither of my parents nor my two brothers were saved at the time. I would cry out for their souls day and night. I could not imagine going to Heaven without them. I would pray and travail often for them. The last time I preached in Pennsylvania before I went to Colorado to take a church in the mountains, my mother raised her hand and gave her life to Christ, thank God. Two years later, she got colon cancer and went to be with the Lord, but I am so grateful to God that she is in Heaven. My dad was an orphan, and he gave his life to Christ a year before my mother did. The first time I shared Jesus with him he said that not only did he not believe in Jesus, but that he didn't believe in God. I was flabbergasted and depressed, so I prayed more fervently in the Spirit.

I know God is great, and He can do these things. As the Holy Spirit would come upon me, I would have this burden for them. Now both of my brothers are saved and serving God. My parents are in Heaven. I was the first Jesus follower in my family, and they thought I was a "Jesus freak" and were worried. I am so grateful to see my whole family in His Kingdom: my son and daughter, our five grandkids, and my brothers and their children also. It has changed our whole family. My original ancestor on my father's side was

Johannes Theodorus Polhemus. He was the first or second pastor in New Amsterdam. (The record is contradictory.) He came to New Amsterdam (New York City) from Brazil by way of the Netherlands. When he came to the United States he pastored there in the 1600s. Immediately his relatives followed Christ, but over the centuries we lost our Christian heritage.

My mother's grandfather was the Pastor of the First Baptist Church of Eufaula, Alabama. Unfortunately his son, her father, was an alcoholic and rejected Christ. He hated his father and the ministry that he felt took his father from him. We had lost our Christian heritage from both family lines, but by the power of the Holy Spirit, God brought it all back. I am very thankful, not just for my own salvation but for my family's salvation. I am thankful that my son is now the executive pastor of our church. The Holy Spirit blows our minds on a continual basis! He does abundantly above what we can think or ask! (Eph. 3:20)

Frances Chan wrote, "I don't want my life to be explainable without the Holy Spirit. I want people to look at my life and know I couldn't be doing this by my own power. I want to live in such a way that I am desperate for Him to come through. That if He doesn't come through, I am screwed." The good news is that He does come through![2]

The Gifts of the Holy Spirit: Often misunderstood, rejected and sometimes abused.

Let's talk about another area of misunderstanding: the gifts of the Spirit. Some people think that the gifts of the Spirit are no longer for today. I will show you in the next chapter how this error arose. You don't have to believe everything I say. Just check the Word and go with that.

I admit that sometimes on TV, and in services of some churches, the gifts will be abused by showy evangelists or pastors. I can understand why people get uptight about this kind of display of the gifts. When people use them to manipulate others to give money or to show off that breaks my heart. That should never be the intention. The gifts of the Spirit are given to us so that we can help other people. We can help people in our own natural ability, we but can help them so much more by teaming up with the Holy Spirit!

"But the manifestation of the Spirit is given to each one for the profit of all." (I Cor. 12:7) Are you an "each one?" The correct answer means that you are not excluded from being able to flow in the gifts of the Spirit. The nine gifts are available to all believers. Paul goes on to say, "But one and the same Spirit works all these things, distributing to each one individually as He wills." So the Holy Spirit is the one that distributes each gift to believers. Of course we also need to be willing to be used by the Holy Spirit. Lots of times, He is willing, but we are not willing. So it takes willingness on His part and ours for the gifts to flow. He is often more willing than we are.

---

[1] *The Leadership Secrets of Billy Graham* by Harold Myra and Marshall Shell. © 2005 by Zondervan, Grand Rapids, MI (pgs 22-24).

[2] *Forgotten God: Reversing Our Tragic Neglect of the Holy Spirit* by Francis Chan and Danae Yankoski, © 2009 By David C. Cook, Colorado Springs, CO.

Section 4:

THE GIFTS OF THE SPIRIT

"Jesus gives us the gift of the Holy Spirit, yet when the Spirit comes,
He is loaded with packages! He desires to release much
more in us and through us than we could ever imagine.
These gifts are given for delivery, not for accumulation.
We receive them to pass them on to others."
- Jack W. Hayford

The Book of Acts demonstrates the nine gifts of the Spirit given by God. There are Revelation Gifts, Power Gifts, and Verbal Gifts. In this section we'll explore what these are so you can unwrap, discover, and begin to apply them to your life.

Chapter 7:

The Gifts of the Spirit

The Apostle Paul mentions nine gifts of the Holy Spirit (I Cor. 12:7-11). These nine gifts are evident all through the Book of Acts. Sadly, many Christians believe that the gifts have passed away or ceased, and that they are not meant for us today. This is called Cessation Theology. Many seminaries teach this and many denominational and evangelical churches have also adopted this position, denying the supernatural power of the Holy Spirit. I will attempt to show you how this teaching arose, and why it is not biblically based.

Ironically, the most powerful reformation in the world had a downside. The Reformation brought a powerful religious and cultural transformation from which we are still seeing positive effects from today in Christianity. This Reformation came at a time when the primary religious institution, the Catholic Church, was going through a dark time in its history. True piety and godliness had sunk to a very low level and the Reformation brought a much needed correction to this while it opened up the possibility for individuals to seek a personal relationship with God without a priest between them. Sadly,

Cessationism also developed out of the Protestant Reformation (1517-1648).

A young Catholic (Augustinian) monk named Martin Luther traveled from Germany to Rome, the "Mecca" of the Christian world at that time. He was deeply disturbed by the debauchery and insincerity of priests and monks in Rome, and he was shocked at the lack of piety and integrity. When he returned to Germany, he found a man named Tetzel selling "Indulgences" in his hometown. He became incensed with righteous anger.

Let me explain: "Indulgences" were sold in order to finance the building of St. Peter's Cathedral in Rome. They could range from one third to one half a year's wages for the average worker, but they would guarantee entrance into Heaven. Not only was this theologically unsound, it was morally corrupt: ensuring that the wealthy had an easy path to Heaven while the poor were doomed to Hell, unable to purchase their "salvation." For Luther this was the "straw that broke the camel's back!" He was already upset with so much of the emphasis being placed on salvation through works, and now people were being told they could buy their way to Heaven! On October 31, 1517 he nailed "The Ninety-Five Theses" to the Wittenberg Chapel door. These were powerful declarations of truth for the most part. There were other reformers like John Calvin and Zwingli who rose up and formed the intellectual backdrop of what became known as the "Protestant Reformation."

The reformers were protesting what was happening in the Catholic Church at the time and were actually trying to reform Catholicism. They emphasized that salvation came only by grace through faith (Eph. 2:8-9). They placed the emphasis back on the finished work of Jesus Christ on the cross, a very important correction. They also emphasized the "priesthood of all believers." The office of priest had been placed on a high pedestal in the Catholic Church. Only he could read scripture; the common believer was prohibited from reading the Bible. He was the only one who could turn the communion elements into the actual body and blood of Jesus Christ (known as transubstantiation). If a priest didn't baptize your baby and it died, you were told it would go to Hell. Tremendous power was placed in the priest's position. The reformers rightly debunked this as well as replacing the Pope's authority and infallibility with the Bible.

These were tumultuous times in the Christian world, and many reformers were persecuted and even martyred because of their stance. Martin Luther was excommunicated by the Catholic Church, and he responded by translating the Bible into German. Thus he was able to give access to the Bible to his people-for the first time they could read it for themselves. What an amazing transformation!

But because the reformers were so set on trying to distance themselves from the Catholic Church, they came against the supernatural aspects of the Holy Spirit such as the "gifts of the Spirit" and "speaking in tongues." The Catholic Church embraced the supernatural and believed in miracles, healing, and the gifts of the Spirit. Sometimes they did this to a fault and even set up shrines and declared some people special "saints" who had operated in the supernatural.

The reformers decided it was best to throw the baby (the supernatural reality) out with the bath water (false doctrines). They came up with a doctrine that said the things of the Spirit were no longer valid. They denounced the present possibility of miracles, "the gifts of the Spirit" and "tongues." They developed a theology which said that these supernatural occurrences- including healing- were only to establish the early church. The reformers taught that after the Bible was canonized all these supernatural aspects "passed away" or "ceased," thus the theology of "Cessationism." Commitment to this belief exerted a strong influence during the Reformation and far beyond.

Cessation theology is still popular today among many Evangelicals especially in the United States. Now these churches usually don't mention Cessationism, but they do not believe in nor do they allow the gifts, healing, or tongues, believing they have passed away. This whole theology is primarily based on only one passage of scripture which makes it shaky to begin with. Doctrinal beliefs should always be considered in context of the whole counsel of God (Acts 20:27).

If possible put aside any bias you may have toward this subject, and imagine you are looking at this passage for the very first time. "Love never fails. But whether there are prophecies, they will fail; whether there are tongues, they will **cease**; whether there is knowledge, it will vanish away. For we know in part and we prophesy in part, but when that which is perfect has come, then that which is in part will be done away. When I was a child, I spoke as a child, I understood as a child, I thought as a child; but when I became a man, I put away childish things. For now we see in a mirror, dimly, but then face to face. Now I know in part, but then I shall know just as I also am known." (I Corinthians 13:8-12 NKJV, emphasis mine).

Now let's allow the passage to speak for itself. Notice where it says "tongues will cease" (from which we get Cessation theology), the question is this: when will tongues cease? Reading further it says "when that which is perfect has come, then that which is in part will be done away." We all would agree that "when that which is perfect has come" refers to a future event, separate from the moment when this text was written. The Cessationists say that "the perfect" refers to the Bible. If you argue this point with them, they will often say "What? You don't believe the Bible is the perfect, infallible, rule of faith?"

To this I would answer, "I absolutely believe the Bible is infallible and serves as our authority and rule of faith," but I question whether 'the perfect' used in the context of this scripture passage refers to the Bible.

As we read on, notice it says; "For now we see in a mirror dimly, but then face to face." In the future, "the perfect" is in parallel with "face to face." Certainly "face to face" can't refer to the Bible. There will clearly be a time when we will see "face to face." Who will we see face to face? The perfect one: Jesus! We will see Him face to face either when He returns or when we go to Heaven. To make this even clearer, the next sentence says, "Now I know in part, but then I shall know just as I also am known." That also is in parallel with "the perfect," and "face to face." There will be a time when we will know as we are known, and it is not here on earth but in Heaven! Thus "the perfect" obviously refers to Jesus, and the timing refers to when we will be with Jesus, face to face, knowing and being known.

Do you think there will be any need for prophecy, tongues, healing or any of the gifts of the Spirit in Heaven? I don't think so! That is why it is sad and unethical when someone uses a "proof text," to support a doctrine. This simply means they take a scripture out of context (a proof text) to back their theological position. When this differs from the true meaning and is clearly taken out of context, it is called "*eisegesis*." When we allow the scripture to be interpreted according to its overall context it is called "exegesis" (critical explanation of a text), which is how biblical passages should be interpreted.

The Cessationists resort to "eisegises" to attempt to support their incorrect position. On close examination of the context one can see clearly that the gifts, prophecy and tongues, etc, will not pass away until we are in Heaven. I am thankful God knew we would need His supernatural help in this age as much as when the church was birthed.

Cessation theology is not based on a biblical foundation. Although it has been accepted in many, many churches in the United States, it is slowly starting to lose its theological hold here. Now, if you go to Asian and African nations, most third world countries, or places of persecution, there is no debate over the Holy Spirit. They are so dependent on Him and God's supernatural power! They know they need the gifts of the Spirit and rely on His supernatural power! There is no question of "is it real?" or "is it for today?" Because they are much more open to the Holy Spirit, they experience many more miracles than we do in this nation. They are hungry for the supernatural power of God.

It is interesting that one of the largest denominations who are strongly cessationist recently changed their position for missionaries allowing them to speak in tongues. Much of their decision was based on seeing how God's supernatural power was rapidly spreading the Gospel and transforming nations around the world. They are now willing to make room for missionaries who believe in tongues, the gifts, and move in the Holy Spirit's empowering even though it doesn't fit their theological structure.

Now that we have settled this important theological issue, we can practically examine the "gifts of the Spirit." I want you to understand that these gifts are available to all believers, not just pastors and evangelists. They are to be used not only in the church world but also in the business world, in education, the arts, government, and all facets of society. These gifts are from God to make us better husbands and wives, fathers and mothers, children, etc. We are made better people over all because we can tap into the Holy Spirit's supernatural ability. I Corinthians 12:7 says, "But the manifestation of the Spirit is given to each one for the profit (benefit) of all." Are you an each one? You bet you are–so you qualify!

Close Examination of the Gifts of the Spirit

For the sake of clarity, in the following chapters I will break down the 9 gifts into three categories:

1. Revelation gifts: Word of Knowledge, Word of Wisdom, Discerning of Spirits

2. Power gifts: Faith, Healings, Miracles

3. Verbal gifts: Tongues, Interpretation of Tongues, Prophecy

"for to one is given the word of wisdom through the Spirit, to another the word of knowledge through the same Spirit, to another faith by the same Spirit, to another gifts of healings by the same Spirit, to another the working of miracles, to another prophecy, to another discerning of spirits, to another different kinds of tongues, to another the interpretation of tongues."
- 1 Corinthians 12:8-10

Chapter 8:

The Revelation Gifts

The revelation gifts are word of knowledge, word of wisdom, and discerning of spirits. These gifts bring insight about people or situations known beyond our natural ability only by the Holy Spirit.

Word of Knowledge

A word of knowledge refers to facts or information received that we cannot know other than by the Holy Spirit. When cowboy Ralph came to the commune he would speak words of knowledge over us. I wouldn't know how he knew these things about me and others. The only possible way was by the power of the Holy Spirit. This had quite an impact on me.

Recently I was on an airplane with an individual and God gave me a word of knowledge about the person sitting next to me. I asked the Holy Spirit how I could bring this word because it was an uncomfortable situation. He told me to bring it in love. So I said to him, "God loves you very much but the person you are involved with outside of your marriage threatens the well being of your family. God is not angry with you but He is concerned over you". He started crying and was just shocked. I was able to pray for him, and he told me it really impacted his life. He was a believer, and when God spoke through me it brought conviction. He told me he was going to do the right thing. It was difficult for me to be obedient-terrifying actually-but the results amazed me! I was so glad I took the risk.

It is important to know the gifts are to be used, wherever you are, not just for church settings. I was in sales for a while, and I walked into this office for a presentation. I was speaking with the CEO, and I kept seeing above him a vision of this kid in my mind. I didn't say — "Well, I was a pastor at one time and I operate in a word of knowledge." However, I did say, "I hope you don't think I am crazy," and then I went on to describe. "He's about 19 years old; he's got dirty blond hair, kind of long and greasy and his jeans are torn and he's got his head down." The CEO starts sobbing quietly. "That's my son, he's strung out on drugs, and he hates my guts." I went around his desk and hugged him and told him my story of how I caused tremendous pain for my dad. I don't think he was a Christian but he told me how much he appreciated my concern and prayer. So I hugged him and left his office.

Later that day I received a voice mail asking me to come back to his office because he was interested in the product I represented. I had totally forgotten about the sale because my heart was primarily to help him. It's really funny. I became the top salesman in that company and I got to speak at sales meetings. They wanted to know how I was so successful. I taught them: "Don't try to sell the person. Just try to help the person. Be honest, and if your product isn't better than what they have, tell them the product they already have is better."

Ironically, I had told some people that their product was better, and they still wanted my products. People will trust you when they know your heart is to help them more than to make the sale for your benefit. This is the secret to being a good salesperson. You probably have experienced times when people are trying hard to sell you. They are pressuring you, and you just want to get the heck out of there.

It was exciting that I got to speak at a national sales meeting, and I told them how important it is to pray, asking God's help, so you will be honest. "Don't try to sell them; try to help them. If you follow this formula you will be a great salesperson, and you will sleep well at night." Caring and helping people, that is what it is all about!

The most dramatic word of knowledge I have ever had was back in 1987. A church had asked me to come to Ft. Morgan, Colorado as an interim pastor. I lived in Greeley and traveled there on weekends. About the fifth or sixth Sunday right in the middle of my message, the Lord impressed on me: "There is somebody here who is planning to kill themselves." There were about 80-100 people there. The Holy Spirit continued to impress me: "They have already written a suicide note, and they are going to kill themselves after the service." I looked out to see if I could see anybody who looked like they were going to commit suicide. Of course, I didn't see anybody who looked distraught, so I didn't bring the word.

I knew 2 Corinthians 5:9 said "we walk by faith and not by sight," but I kept preaching. It was a great message. It was about Gideon, and I was really into it. But, the Lord kept bringing that word stronger and stronger. Finally, I closed my Bible. I decided I was going to obey God. "There is somebody here who has written a suicide note. You are planning to commit suicide after the service." Silence. One minute went by. Two minutes. And, it seemed like days went by.

My mind was thinking, *Well, you aren't going to be asked back here again. You ruined a really good message.*

So I am just standing there; I felt like I am out on a limb that is cracking and about to break. I am going to fall a long way! I sensed the devil mocking me, but felt like I just couldn't go on. All of a sudden, a guy named Joe, in his late twenties, comes walking out of the sound booth, and comes down to the front. As he was coming I could sense a spirit of suicide on him. I came off the stage and broke it over him. He fell down on the floor. Then he got up and turned to people and said: "It is true. I was going to commit suicide this morning. I wrote the suicide note". You could have heard a pin drop–all eyes were on Joe. "But I remembered," he continued, "that I had signed up to do the sound…so I thought I would do the sound first and then go commit suicide."

Joe raised both hands, tears running down his face and he said, "But you know what? The devil's a liar, and I'm free! I'm free!"

Nobody remembers the incredible message I preached that day, but everybody will remember that moment because God showed Himself strong by the power of the Holy Spirit. I am so glad I obeyed. What if I had not? What if somebody had called me later that day and said, "By the way, Joe committed suicide!" I would have felt horrendously bad, and so I am grateful the Holy Spirit would not let me get away with ignoring Him. Thank God He kept pressing me to act. It is so important to be led by the Spirit!

The Word of Wisdom

A word of wisdom is actually the application of knowledge by the Holy Spirit. In Acts 6 we are told that the Hebrews and the Gentiles were going at it. The Gentiles felt that their widows were not being treated as well as the Hebrews. Satan saw an opportunity to split the church along ethnic lines. This would have been devastating to the early church and would have set them back significantly. A Word of Wisdom came to those praying about the situation that they should appoint the first deacons then they would take care of the business while the apostles would keep preaching the Word and ministering. God wanted the apostles to keep doing the work of the ministry and let the deacons handle the logistics at hand. This word of wisdom saved the church from going through an ethnic split by delegating business responsibilities. Thank God for the gifts of the Spirit! He still gives wisdom for difficult situations today.

A few years ago a business man from our church approached me and asked me to pray about a situation. He wanted to buy a friend's business (who was also a Christian), but worried he didn't have the finances. God gave me a word of wisdom about how he could do this. I explained that he would buy the business over a three year period. His friend would mentor him, and it would cut down on his friend's yearly capital gains saving him taxes. Also, it would take the financial pressure off.

He went and talked with his friend who eagerly accepted these terms. Today the business is thriving. Thank God for the wisdom of the Holy Spirit!

Discerning of Spirits

There are three areas of discerning of spirits. One is the Holy Spirit. You have probably operated in this gift at one time without realizing it. Maybe you have been in a worship service, and though you can't see the Holy Spirit, you sure can feel Him. He is there and

His presence is so strong, you know it is the Holy Spirit-this is discerning the Spirit.

The second area of discerning of spirits is the demonic; demons or demonic spirits. I imagine many of you have operated in this gift also without being aware of it. For example you walk into a room and the hair on the back of your neck stands up. You can feel evil all around you. You can't see it, but you can sense it. That's discerning of demonic spirits.

There is a third one and that is discerning of the human spirit. Possibly you may have experienced this also. You meet someone for the first time, and they don't have a cross around their neck or a T-Shirt that says "Jesus," but you sense that they are a Christian. How did you know that? You discerned their human spirit. So, there is discernment of the Holy Spirit, of demonic spirits, and of the human spirit.

Maybe there has been a situation where you are talking to somebody, it might be a business deal and you feel a major uneasiness deep down. You may heed it or you may blow it off, but you feel there is something wrong. That is usually a discerning of the human spirit. You have no reason not to trust them, but against all rationality internally you don't trust that person. Why? Because they are distrustful. I have learned the hard way to trust this prompting of the Holy Spirit and not follow reasoning. This is not easy to do, and I have at times ignored the prompting of the Holy Spirit and gone with my own reasoning. Bad decision. Live and learn!

We have examined three areas of revelation: word of knowledge, word of wisdom and discerning of spirits. Let's move on to the next grouping, the power gifts.

Chapter 9:

The Power Gifts

The power gifts are faith, healing, and miracles.

Faith

The Gift of Faith can appear when you least expect it. Remember I told you the story about the guy who tried to kill me? I was trying to learn to flow in the Holy Spirit and to help people. It was during a Sunday night service, and I had only been out of seminary for less than a year. I was learning to move in the gifts and said, "There is somebody here with a spirit of infirmity. Please come forward." I had seen in my mind an x-ray of somebody bent over and I had heard the words, "a spirit of infirmity." I didn't even know what that meant, but I knew it was in the King James Bible so I figured it was okay to say. Nobody came forward for awhile. All of a sudden a guy in a black leather jacket, who I had never seen before, started walking down the aisle. He was stocky with dark hair. He had a large build, and he came bent over and limping up to the front. He was a young guy, probably 30 or so.

As he came forward, I wondered what to do next because they don't teach you that in seminary. Basically, I remember that there was some oil on the piano, so I grabbed the oil, closed my eyes (because I wanted to look spiritual) and I started to anoint him with the oil. All of a sudden, I opened my eyes and he was going berserk as he came toward me. Surprisingly, I didn't get scared. That seemed strange because I should have been terrified. I believed that a supernatural gift of faith came on me in that moment. I remember yelling authoritatively: "In the name of Jesus I command you to stop"

As soon as I said that, he fell on the ground. I remember thinking, *Wow this actually works. I have authority*. Sometimes you have to learn authority in the trenches.

When he fell on the ground, a couple of elders jumped on him. One of them was a big biker guy named Steve. When Steve acted, other people jumped on him too and we had a deliverance service right there. I wouldn't recommend this on a Sunday night service. It is definitely not "seeker sensitive." I had never seen such a dramatic demonic manifestation. He spoke in these eerie, deep voices as I commanded the demons to loose him. A lady named Carol, had brought her husband Phil to the service. He was not saved and was in the second row. His eyes were bulging out of his head. It literally scared the "hell" out of him. He gave his life to Jesus two weeks later!

So we prayed for this man for about an hour. The next morning there was a knock on my door. It was this same guy but his countenance was totally different, I hardly recognized him! "I want to thank you so much. I was headed to Arizona and just passing through Colorado, but I am so glad I did. After what happened, last night was the first night in a long while I was able to sleep through the night without being tormented."

He told me about how he had been in and out of mental institutions and had been troubled his whole life. I looked at him amazed and said, "Let's thank Jesus together because, to be honest, I really didn't know what I was doing, but the Holy Spirit did know. God did an amazing thing for you." I will never forget that night.

We have all been given a measure of faith (Romans 12:3), but there are other times when we need the release of supernatural faith. There have been times in Pakistan when I needed the "gift of faith" because, otherwise, I would have had the "gift of fear." You don't need fear from the enemy when you are handling difficult situations. When I was in Pakistan earlier this year, it was very tense because of recent church bombings by radicals. We were driving through the area and Leif Hetland said I slept through six tense check points. That's supernatural peace. God is good! Even though we had machine gun body guards, there is no peace like God's peace!

Healings

What about the gift of healings? Notice the word healings is plural because there are a lot of ways that people get healed since healing happens in different areas of their lives. Some need physical healing, others need emotional or relational healing, etc. One way God heals is through the spiritual gifts of healings. Before you can activate this gift, it helps tremendously to first settle in your mind if it is God's will to heal or not.

I am convinced it is God's will to heal. Here's how I know it. Look at the Garden of Eden: no sickness or disease. Then I look at Heaven where there will be no need for healing: physical, emotional financial, relational, etc... There will be no sickness or disease in

Heaven and that represents God's perfect will. But we are not there yet. Now we live on earth in a fallen world.

Why doesn't everyone get healed? Even when it is God's will people often don't get healed. Why? We don't know exactly why, but we keep pressing in for healing anyway. You probably think when you get to Heaven, you will ask God, "Why didn't so-and-so get healed?" But when you get to Heaven, you won't care because every believer will be whole with a new body. From Heaven's perspective whether a person lived 8 years or 80, it will seem very short in terms of eternity!

Jesus walked on this earth and healed many people. He never told anyone, "Go my Father has made you sick so you will gain spiritual insight." The Holy Spirit brought healing power through Him. He is the healer and was the embodiment of God's will.

The Holy Spirit releases His healing power through us. Thus, this gift can operate through any believer by the power of the Holy Spirit. Sometimes I will feel a tangible anointing of His healing power on my hands. Other times, I won't feel anything, but it doesn't seem to matter. Sometimes, people get healed whether I feel a tangible anointing or not. You can't go by external manifestations of the Spirit. I believe He allows us to feel a tangible anointing to encourage us and to help counter our unbelief and fear. Now we train many people in our healing ministry because the Holy Spirit wants to flow through all believers not just special ones.

One of the most miraculous healings I've seen was at a healing conference at our church with Randy Clark, Bill Johnson, and Leif Hetland. All three of these men walk in a very strong healing anointing. Yet the greatest miracle at that conference was a young boy about five years old who couldn't walk. He would drag his leg with his arms on crutches. Two teenage girls prayed for him, and he ran across the stage to a crying mother. Incredible! God wants to use any of us who are willing.

There are many types of healings besides physical. I have seen Christian counselors as well as regular believers get incredible insight from the Holy Spirit resulting in emotional healing for someone. Remember Jesus said He came "to heal the broken hearted" (emotional healing) ((Luke 4:18 NKJV).. Deliverance is another area of healing where people are set free, by the Holy Spirit. In the same verse Jesus says that He came "to set at liberty those who are oppressed" (Luke 4:18).

The Gift of Miracles

Miracles are occurrences that can't be explained through natural law. I have seen more miracles in third world countries because it seems people are more desperate there. However, we are now seeing many more miracles here in the U.S. We have Healing Rooms at our church. We just witnessed a little baby healed dramatically. The parents thought their baby was going to have to have surgery for a serious brain tumor, but instead was miraculously healed. Another person was radically healed of stage four cancer. The doctor said "I can't understand it. I'd say it is a miracle." All throughout the book of Acts the Holy Spirit performed miracles through the believers. It is still happening today!

There are times when the power gifts (faith, healings and miracles), can all be operating simultaneously. The beginning of Acts 3 there is a story about a lame man who would sit at the gate of the temple begging for alms. Peter grabs the man by the hand and lifts him up saying "In the name of Jesus rise up and walk." This man was immediately healed and went away "walking and leaping and praising God" (Acts 3:1-10).

I believe there were three power gifts working in this case: the gift of faith (it took faith for Peter to lift him to his feet); the gift of healings (physical healing manifested immediately); and the gift of miracles (this man had been lame since birth). What a great example from the Bible of common men like Peter and John operating in all these gifts at once.

Not everyone we pray for gets healed, which I confess is disappointing, but I will not quit praying for healing for people just because some didn't receive healing. Rather than becoming discouraged let's continue to press forward, even when we don't understand the why or why not?

Chapter 10:

The Verbal Gifts

The verbal gifts are speaking in tongues, interpretation and prophesy.

The Gift of Tongues

The gift of tongues is when a message is given in a language that is not understood by the speaker or hearer. It is given by the Holy Spirit to others. It is a gift, so it is to help the person or persons it is addressed to. However, this gift needs to be accompanied by the gift of interpretation.

Gift of Interpretation of Tongues

The gift of the interpretation of tongues is the Holy Spirit's conveying understanding of the given word in tongues into the person or persons own language. These two gifts bring edification to the person or group of people the message is intended for. Remember the gifts are always to help others. Unfortunately in the Corinthian church there was bewilderment as people were just praying in tongues without interpretation. This brought confusion (which Paul attempted to clear up in 1 Cor. 14). We will talk more about tongues later.

Prophesy

To prophesy means to speak forth what the Holy Spirit reveals. "He who prophesies speaks edification, exhortation and comfort to people." (1 Cor. 14:3) Prophesy at times has been misused to condemn or manipulate people. Remember the word makes it clear it should be encouraging, exhorting, and/or comforting. Prophecy is something all believers can flow in. You don't have to be a prophet, any believer can prophesy (1 Cor. 14:31). Thus it is very different from the Old Testament where primarily only prophets or kings prophesied. In fact, the New Testament says, "We prophecy in part" (1 Cor. 13:9). So if someone brings you a prophetic word and it contradicts God's word, reject it. If it is not encouraging, or comforting or exhorting reject it. If that word doesn't make sense, don't act on it. Put it on a back burner in your life and ask the Holy Spirit to confirm it now or down the road. Usually prophesy can be very powerful and encouraging. Sometimes prophecy even gives a glimpse into our future.

Like all spiritual gifts, prophecy isn't just for church. I have been on airplanes, and God has spoken something to me, words of encouragement that I have been able to bring to strangers. Sometimes it brings them to Christ. Sometimes, it brings them to a place where they are more open to Him. We have children and youth who go out into the market place. They do "treasure hunts," where they seek the Holy Spirit and get words or pictures. They may get the color of the person's sweater, or a kind of hat they are wearing. (Sometimes they may even get the name of the person). When they see someone who meets that description they will share with them what God is saying.

Children cause people to drop their defenses. When a child explains what they received from the Holy Spirit, often people will break down crying with joy. The children get to them in an amazing way. You don't have to be a child to operate in the gift of prophecy. The Holy Spirit will show you things about people to bless them. We don't bring up horrible things. That's not God and certainly isn't love. He brings up good things, and we teach people to always operate in love. If a person shares where a person is struggling, they will do it in such a way that rather than condemn them, it encourages and strengthens them to move toward victory. In John 4 Jesus meets a Samaritan woman at a well. He tells her she has been married several times and the man she is living with is not her husband. But He has living water for her. He does it in such love that she is blown away and tells her whole neighborhood, "Come see the man who has told me all about myself." That is the power of prophesy delivered in love.

Below is a powerful example of how a prophetic outreach was carried out, written in his own words.

Chicago Story by Zachary Spector (Youth Pastor of The Rock)

> In July of 2014 our youth ministry went on a mission trip to inner city Chicago. Our team consisted of 15 students ranging from sixth to twelfth grade. Our trip offered numerous opportunities to serve the city of Chicago in different ways. While God did many things on that trip, there was one particular encounter that stood out above the rest. We did a spiritual treasure hunt which is the application of receiving a word

of knowledge or prophecy from God and then delivering it to the person He highlights.

On our final day in Chicago we split into teams of four and drove to the downtown area. We asked the Holy Spirit for some pictures of people to talk to and pray for. Our team came up with a list of 18 different descriptions of people. Some of the things on that list were: African American with a red shirt, black male with headphones and dreadlocks, along with many others.

As we were walking around the city, our time was spent unsuccessfully searching for any who fit this description. We were discouraged, disappointed, and displeased with the way our last hour had gone. When we reached the point of giving up and calling it quits, we saw a man who identically resembled one of the people God had shown us earlier: tall, black male, about 6'3", big headphones that covered his ears, dreadlocks, and a red shirt! Even though I was the leader, insecurities and indecision left me skeptical about approaching the man. It took a middle school student to go up to him.

We approached him unassumingly and asked if we could talk to him for a minute. We told him that while we were driving down to the city, we asked God to give us a picture of someone who needs His touch and told him that he was the man God had shown us. We told him "God so deeply loves you and regardless of what you are going through, God has a plan and hope for your life that is greater than you can imagine." After talking to him, our middle school student asked, "Can we pray for you?"

"Sure," he shrugged, and we held hands.

As she was praying, we could feel a lightness come over us. It was as if something was being loosed. As the prayer continued, tears began pouring down this big tough man's face. When we finished praying, he looked up and said, "Just minutes before you approached me I was on the phone with my best friend..." his voice trailed.

More tears came and before he continued in almost a whisper, "I was planning and plotting my own suicide...I had lost all hope," he stammered, "I told my friend that unless something miraculous happened, I was going to end my life...your obedience spared my life...you will never know how much it means."

You can imagine how this encounter changed the life of everyone involved. It was a demonstration of the Holy Spirit's power at work in and through us. It showed us that obedience is always worth the cost. It made us aware that God wants to use us to be His hands and feet to others. Don't ever underestimate a moment when the Holy Spirit is involved!

Be led by the Spirit

The good news is that we get to be led by the Spirit, and we get to impact people's lives! Sometimes it may be a person at work who you sense is going through something emotionally. You may put your arm around them and offer to pray for them. You can't believe how that impacts a person's life. People don't care how much you know until they know how much you care.

Think of the early disciples. They followed Jesus and thought He would reign as a political king, freeing them from the tyranny of Roman rule, heavy taxation, and unfair treatment of the Jews. They even argued who would be at His right and left hand. They wanted to be his Prime Minister and rule with Him on earth. Then all of a sudden, He is crucified, the most disgraceful way a person could die. They just didn't get it. They hid for fear that they would be next to die!

Imagine you were one of those early disciples and Jesus tells you that you have to go out and convince a skeptical world that knows He has been crucified, that Jesus is alive! You know you aren't going to do it through great oratory. You are only going to do it if the Holy Spirit shows up to lead you, and brings signs and wonders with Him!.

"And the disciples went everywhere and preached,
and the Lord worked through them, confirming what they said
by many miraculous signs."
- Mark 16:20 NLT

I have found that going into Pakistan, and trying to verbally convince Muslims that they need Jesus does not work. You first have to have love for them. Leif Hetland has told me many times, "If you don't have love for those Muslims, you are never going to reach them. It doesn't matter how powerful you think you are in the Spirit." We also need to demonstrate His love. We have seen many miraculous things happen there. Thank God, He still accompanies His followers with signs and wonders!

There are times we all need to risk being obedient to His leading. If we are unwilling to fail, we will never succeed. It is better to be a "wet water walker than a dry boat sitter." Remember the story of when Peter jumped out of the boat in obedience to Jesus' promptings. I am sure the guys back in the boat were making fun of him. Peter actually walked on the water, and then when he looked at the waves, he went under. I am sure the other disciples were ridiculing him. Jesus, with His arms of mercy, reached out and picked Peter from the water. Peter made it to Jesus!

The guys back in the boat could only criticize. Guess who got to preach on the Day of Pentecost? Even after he had denied Jesus three times, it was Peter!. He was a risk taker. He was not afraid. He was willing to step out of the boat, and even when he messed up and was forgiven he didn't come under condemnation. He experienced the loving grace of His Father. God used him mightily to see 3,000 plus people come into the Kingdom on the day of Pentecost! *"For all who are led by the Spirit of God are the children of God."* (Romans 8:14 NLT) He so desires us to be led by His Spirit!

Francis Chan, the mega church pastor who realized how much he needed the Holy Spirit writes: "*We are scared to make mistakes, so we fret over figuring out God's will. We wonder how living according to His will actually looks and feels and we are scared to find out. We forget that we were never promised a twenty year plan of action; instead God promises multiple times in scripture never to leave or forsake us. God wants us to listen to His Spirit on a daily basis, and even throughout the day, and different and stretching moments arise, and in the midst of the mundane my hope is that instead of searching for "God's will in my life," each of us would learn to seek hard after "the Spirit's leading in my life today."* [1]

I pray that you and I would be led by the Spirit daily. To be honest sometimes I know I am being led by the Holy Spirit, but other times I am led by my own feelings or intellect. It is then that I miss it. The Lord will try to direct me, but I get distracted. So cut yourself some slack. We are human, we're not perfect, but we are growing. As we learn how to walk in the Spirit, He helps us, He guides us, He is with us. He is in us, and He loves us even when we fail trying to obey!

"Father, I thank you for each and every person and pray that we will all be led by your Spirit on a daily, moment by moment basis. Thank you that you are available to us 24/7. You never leave us; you never forsake us. Help us Father to make a difference in this world. Help us to make a difference in the lives of others and let your love consume us and move us beyond our comfort zones. In Jesus' name. Amen"

Getting to Know the Holy Spirit

Before we can get into how the Holy Spirit imparts to us, it is essential to build a relationship with Him. The Holy Spirit is the part of the Godhead that we have direct contact with. Remember God the Father is in Heaven and God the Son is seated at His right hand. But the Holy Spirit is right here on earth. When we say that we sense God's presence, it is the Holy Spirit we are sensing.

Frances Chan was the pastor of a 20,000 member evangelical church but became dissatisfied with the lack of transformation going on. He saw programs adding numbers but not changing lives. He realized that what was lacking was the presence of the Holy Spirit and writes: *"The Holy Spirit is absolutely vital to our situation today. Of course, He is always vital; but perhaps especially now. After all, if the Holy Spirit moves, nothing can stop Him." If He doesn't move, we will not produce genuine fruit – no matter how much effort or money we expend. The church becomes irrelevant when it becomes purely a human effort or money we expend. The church becomes irrelevant when it becomes purely a human creation. We are not all we were made to be when everything in our lives and churches can be explained apart from the work and presence of the Holy Spirit."*[1]

Perhaps some people are mystified by the Holy Spirit because He is invisible. People can visualize Jesus or imagine God, but the Holy Spirit seems elusive. This is not true. Jesus talked all about the Holy Spirit just before He went to the cross trying to get His disciples and us to understand how vital He is to our lives.

Jesus made it clear that it was better to have the Holy Spirit with them than for Him to remain there. They probably didn't believe Him until after He died, resurrected and sent the Holy Spirit. "Nevertheless I tell you the truth. It is to your advantage that I go away; for if I do not go away, the Helper will not come to you; but if I depart, I will send Him to you." (John 16:7)

Don't be afraid of building a relationship with the Holy Spirit. Just as God desires intimacy with you wanting to be called "Abba" (a term even more intimate than our word "Daddy") (see Romans 8:15) so does the Holy Spirit, Jesus wants that same intimacy with us. He said: *"No longer do I call you servants, for a servant does not know what his master is doing; but I have called you friends, for all things that I heard from My Father I have made known to you."* (John 15:15)

Remember He is one God: Father, Son and Holy Spirit. So how do we get better acquainted with the Holy Spirit? By prayer; by waiting on Him; by soaking in His presence; by allowing Him to make the Word come alive; by fellowshipping with other believers; and the list goes on!

The most important part of our relationship with Him is the receiving part. Allowing Him to download or impart to us. So next let's talk about impartation and the many ways the Holy Spirit does this.

---

[1] *Forgotten God by Francis Chan* and Danae Yankoske. © 2009 by David C. Cook, Colorado Springs, CO.

Section 5

IMPARTATION: HOW THE HOLY SPIRIT COMMUNICATES WITH US

"You might as well try to see without eyes, hear without ears, or breathe without lungs, as to try to live the Christian life without the Holy Spirit"
- D.L. Moody

The Holy Spirit has many ways of impartation: through His Word; through dreams and visions; through other believers; through the still, small voice; through divine revelation; and through our own spirit once made alive in Christ. How we receive impartation from the Holy Spirit and how we release it to others can change the world.

Chapter 11:

How the Holy Spirit Communicates With Us

In this chapter we will discuss the primary ways the Holy Spirit communicates with us. Let us never limit Him saying He has to do it on our terms because there are many ways He imparts to us. All are valid, all are valuable, yet each is unique.

The Word

Have you ever been reading the Word of God and something seems to just leap off the page and come alive? You may have read this passage before, but suddenly it takes on a new meaning that applies directly to your life. When this happens it is the Holy Spirit making God's word "*rhema*" or revelation to you. There are two Greek words in the original language in the New Testament translated "word." One is "*logos*" which means the "written word." The other word is "*rhema*" which means the "revealed word." The Holy Spirit turns "logos" (written) into "rhema" (revealed).

While I was in seminary, we had this old Peugeot that kept breaking down. We were struggling with one child and another on the way, so we had no money to get another car. My father-in-law gave us $2,000 toward a car. I saw a car advertised at Reedman's Auto Mart which was the largest car dealer in the world at the time. They had a huge clock in front of the dealership which would "bong" every 3-1/2 minutes. That was how often they sold a car.

In the paper I saw a Dodge Colt station wagon advertised for $2,000, the exact price matching my means, but I had been told never to buy a used car from Reedman's. The salesman told me that someone else was also interested, but he would give me until 9:00 am in the morning to decide. I tossed and turned praying for wisdom. The Holy Spirit directed me to get up, go into the bathroom and turn to Mark 11. Amazingly this passage instructed the disciples to go into the neighboring town and get a "colt" (where else in the Bible do you find that word?) and say the master had need of it. That was funny because the dealership was in a neighboring town. To make a long story short I purchased the car. It turned out to be a great car, and I never had a problem with it. When I graduated from seminary, I gave it to someone who was going to Bible School. I heard they gave it to someone else when they graduated. For all I know, it may still be taking students through school!

God used His Word uniquely to answer the question I put before Him, "Should I buy this car or not?" The passage the Holy Spirit highlighted provided clear confirmation that allowed me to act in faith. Time itself proved that the decision was wise and that I had indeed heard from God on the matter.

Dreams and Visions

Another way the Holy Spirit communicates with us is through dreams and visions. Several years ago I was planning to go to Tibet. Our church had adopted the Kham Tibetans who were an unreached people group of nomads. There were no Christians in their tribe at that time. This was about 15 years ago. I had this dream or vision, I don't remember which. Scripture says "old men dream dreams" so it was probably a dream! In the dream I was in a room with light coming through a window and I was there with the "Living" Buddha, who was the head of the Buddhist monastery. Also, I was sharing the Gospel, in a non-combative way.

A few weeks later I went to Tibet with a group from our church. We had a translator and a tracker. The translator said he had an opportunity to go with just two people to the Bone Monastery, where foreigners had never gone before in over 2,000 years. He said it was very dangerous to get there, but I remembered my dream, and I knew I had to go. He told us that we would have to ride horses part of the time, and there were sheer cliffs that dropped off. Only one other guy from the team had the courage to go, and he was good with horses. So, the horseman, the tracker, the translator and I made the trek. My horse fell down in the water once, but fortunately wasn't hurt. The cliffs were steep and treacherous, so a false move would mean death. We climbed 14,000 feet to get to the monastery. The air was thin and clear, so that night the stars were the brightest I had ever seen.

There were 100 monks living at this monastery. The head monk, ("Living Buddha") gave us a private audience the first day, and I shared the Gospel with him just as I had in the dream. I would never have done so but the dream encouraged me.. He had heard the Gospel on the radio when he lived in Beijing, so he was really open to it. That night he came to my room, and we spoke for three hours. He believed in reincarnation and told me that he sensed he had known me in past lives. The Bible doesn't teach reincarnation, but I knew God was stirring the heart of this monk and that this was a divine appointment. I was able to tell him about my own experience as a Zen Buddhist at the Monterey Zendo in California. I shared how Jesus had come into my life, and how it was like going from two dimensions to three because now I had a personal relationship with God through Jesus. He was not defensive at all; in fact he was very receptive.

Not every dream is from God. Sometimes it may be from eating too much pizza before bed, but I knew my dream was from God. Even the room where we first met was exactly like the room in the dream. The Holy Spirit revealed this to me while I was sleeping. Had He not given me that vision, I would never have taken that dangerous trip up a mountain in Tibet, nor been bold enough to share the Gospel with a Buddhist monk. Just as His Word had confirmed my decision about the car, this dream guided my decisions to go up the mountain and speak with the monk.

Through other believers

The Holy Spirit can also speak to us through other people. Several times in my life I have had prophetic words spoken to me which brought great encouragement. I remember a few years ago when we were battling to get approval for our church to build on our new land and things were not going well. A man came to the warehouse where our church met, and said God had clearly shown him we would be building a church. He told me the area he had seen and said it would be as a "lighthouse" to the area. This greatly encouraged me at the time since this was the same area the Holy Spirit had shown me. Bob

Hazlett, a man with a strong prophetic gift, gave me a very encouraging word recently about my future. This actually kept me from stepping down from ministry at a very discouraging time in my life.

The Still Small Voice

One of the most important methods the Holy Spirit uses to communicate with us directly is by a "still small voice."

Things which occur in the Old Testament are often a shadow of the New Testament fulfillment to come. There is an impactful story about Elijah found in 1 Kings 19. Though he had just won an incredible victory over the Baal worshipers, he got deeply depressed soon after. He retreated to a cave where he was hiding in fear from a woman named Jezebel. The Lord told him to come out of his cave and stand on the mountain before Him. "Behold, the Lord passed by. And a great and strong wind tore into the mountain and broke the rocks in pieces before the Lord" (v. 11). Now, it is interesting that a lot of people look for God in the dramatic, but often when we look for Him in the demonstrative; we miss Him at work in the subtle or the non-dramatic.

The Lord can come to us dramatically, but often does not. The same passage goes on to say that the Lord was not in the wind and after the wind there was an earthquake. But, the Lord was not in the earthquake either. After the earthquake, there was a fire. Now, every child of Israel knew that God often showed up in a fire. Hadn't Moses encountered Him in the "burning bush"? Hadn't God led them through the wilderness by a "pillar of fire" at night? So they knew that God could show up by fire. But God wasn't in the fire.

The Word says that after the fire, there was a "still small voice." That's where God was! In the Hebrew the literal meaning is not "still" but "silent." So the actual translation should be a "silent, small voice." That didn't make sense to the translators, so they put it in a way that made more sense. I am sure they were thinking, "How can you have a silent voice?" But that really is how the Holy Spirit often communicates with us. I have never heard an audible voice, but I often hear Him in a silent, small voice.

In the Book of John, Jesus talks about the important role that Holy Spirit will play after He was gone. "When the spirit of truth comes, he will guide you into all truth. He will not speak on his own but will tell you what he has heard. He will tell you about the future." (John 16:13 NLT) Jesus was trying to get the disciples to understand that they would be much better off with the Holy Spirit. The Holy Spirit would guide, lead, and direct them. The primary way the Holy Spirit leads today is by the "silent, small voice." The Amplified Bible says "a sound of gentle stillness." Listen and you'll hear it too.

Revelation

Right after the Apostle Paul explained that he didn't come to the Corinthians in his own eloquence, but that he trusted in the power of the Holy Spirit so their faith would be in the same. He goes on to explain: "But as it is written, 'Eye has not seen, nor ear heard, nor have entered into the heart of man the things which God has prepared for those who love Him." (1 Cor. 2:9). A lot of people stop here. They may use this passage to rationalize when they don't understand what is going on. But that is not where the scripture stops. It goes on to say, "But God has revealed them to us through his Spirit...for the Spirit searches all things, yes, the deep things of God. For what man knows the things of a man except the spirit of the man which is in him?" (v. 10-11) Notice, the small "s" is referring to the human spirit.

It is the Holy Spirit bringing revelation directly to the human spirit. "Even so no one knows the things of God except the Spirit of God. Now we have received, not the spirit of the world, but the Spirit who is from God… that we might know the things that have been freely given to us by God." (v.12)

So remember the Holy Spirit comes and imparts things from God to us. The good news is that you received the Holy Spirit when you received Jesus Christ as Lord and Savior–you already have Him living inside you. All believers have access to this revelation even if they don't realize it or choose not to receive it.

God is in Heaven, Jesus is at the right hand of the Father, but the Holy Spirit is the primary one who communicates with us on earth: "These things we also speak, not in words which man's wisdom teaches but which the Holy Spirit teaches, comparing spiritual things with spiritual. (In other words, the Holy Spirit brings revelation unto our human spirit.) But the natural man does not receive the things of the Spirit of God, for they are foolishness to him; nor can he know them because they are spiritually discerned." (vs. 13-14) The natural man refers both to the individual who is not "born again" and to the soulish part of the believer that is guided by mind and emotions. Satan or demons can speak into our mind but not into the human spirit of a believer. This should help when we are trying to discern whether it is God, Satan or ourselves that we are hearing.

Spirit to Human Spirit Impartation

Before we received Jesus Christ, the Holy Spirit was not able to penetrate our human spirit because it was not yet alive unto God. There was a blockage, but Jesus was the one who opened that up so we could receive from the Holy Spirit. Notice it says the "natural" man cannot receive the things of the Holy Spirit. Why? When you are "born again," what part of you comes alive? It is your spirit;–not your body. I was going bald when I got saved and now I am really bald. I didn't get a new head of hair (my body did not change). But my mind, will, and emotions would gradually be changed and impacted by the Word of God. My spirit was instantly changed, but it took time for my mind and emotions to reflect the change.

It says in Romans, "be transformed by the renewing of your mind." So the Word revealed by the Holy Spirit renews our mind and our emotions. It helps our will to line up with His will. Yet it is our human spirit that is instantaneously made alive at our "new birth" and that is the place we receive revelation. Sometimes that impartation is visual, sometimes it is audible, and sometimes we feel it or sense it. Our senses pick up on the reception after it is transmitted to our human spirit.

Where is the Physical Center of the Human Spirit?

Believe it or not the Bible teaches that the physical center of the human spirit is our abdomen! (Some of you have more of the Spirit than others!) "The spirit of a man is the lamp of the Lord, searching all the inner depths of the heart." (Prov. 20:27) The King James Version translates this as "belly" instead of "heart." The King James Version is sometimes antiquated in its language, but here it is much closer to the meaning in the original language. The literal Hebrew translation here is "rooms of the belly" or abdomen. This is very important to understand. You will be able to receive impartation in a much clearer way if you understand this truth, even if at first it doesn't make sense to you.

Eastern culture seems to understand this concept far better than we Westerners. We usually see the brain as our center not the abdomen. When I teach at YWAM bases, I sometimes encounter Korean students who have no trouble at all with this concept. The translation of their Bible is much closer to the original language, so "rooms of the belly" was not at all strange for them.

Jesus makes this truth even more apparent. "He who believes in Me, as the scripture has said, out of his heart will flow rivers of living water. But this He spoke concerning the Spirit, whom those believing in Him would receive, for the Holy Spirit was not yet given, because Jesus was not yet glorified." (John 7:38-39) Jesus was speaking of a time when He would no longer be hanging out with them. When He would be glorified, He would be sending the Holy Spirit. Notice He says: "out of your "Koilia" would flow rivers of living water. "Koilia" is the Greek word from which we get the English word colon.

When the Holy Spirit imparts something to us, it is to our human spirit whose physical center is our abdomen! Have you ever said, "I have a gut feeling about that." Often it is the Holy Spirit bringing revelation. Sadly, our reasoning often tries to override what we are receiving from the Holy Spirit. This has gotten me into trouble because it doesn't seem to make sense to my mind, so I reject it.

In October of 2012 Graham Cooke spoke at our church and brought a powerful prophetic word to our congregation and to the leaders from other churches in Colorado. He told of a coming move of the Spirit where "The (spiritual) water level would be rising and that God would take off the roof" (of spiritual hindrances).This seemed too good to be true to my natural reasoning. Ironically, we saw this in the natural when a wind and hail storm tore into our roof-causing damaging leaks and the water level to rise in the sanctuary!

But in the Spirit we began to experience open Heavens and a greater move of the Spirit. In Graham's word there was a warning that we must put away the sectarian, competitive spirit and work together in unity for this to happen. When my son came on as Executive Pastor in 2014, he began creating great unity among the pastors and churches in our community. Since then God has brought amazing reformation to our community. We just had the 2nd annual Castle Rock Day of Prayer with over 25 pastors and leaders and even more churches represented. The presence of God was tangible.

Also, we and other churches are reaching out and helping the hurting, the homeless, and those struggling. Many are coming into His Kingdom as the Presence grows stronger. His word is coming to pass despite my skepticism. Praise God!

So we have discussed how the Holy Spirit speaks to us through His Word; through dreams and visions, through other believers; through the still, small voice; through divine revelation; and through our own spirit once made alive to Christ. In the next chapter I will share further personal experiences with you of how the Holy Spirit has spoken to, guided, directed, and protected me.

Chapter 12:

Put to the Test

A Former Youth Pastor Tries to Oust Me

When I first came to The Rock as the lead pastor, a youth pastor was already on staff. He seemed like a good guy and could preach well. I would have him preach when I was gone or needed a break. Even though he did well, I felt an uneasiness concerning him. Something seemed off, but I couldn't figure out what it was. Reasoning would say "You are being paranoid, get over it." And I would think, "What's wrong with me? I really shouldn't think badly of this person."

Then one evening a young couple asked if they could meet with me privately. They went on to tell me that this youth pastor was secretly going to people (we were very small at that time only about 50 – 70 people) and telling them they needed to vote me out.

It suddenly made sense. Sure enough he felt overlooked and believed he was God's man for the head pastor job. Wow, I realized the Holy Spirit had been attempting to warn me, but I would blow it off by my reasoning. I confronted the youth pastor and all hell broke loose. I rode out the storm and helped him find a job as a pastor at a rural church about 20 miles away. If only I had listened to the promptings of the Holy Spirit, I could have headed this off sooner with less fallout. This was a hard lesson for me, but a valuable one.

Ironically, when I was a Zen Buddhist, we were taught when meditating to center down into the abdomen (called the "harrah"). Buddhists understand the center of our being is not the intellect but the abdomen. Zen Buddhists understand this truth better than most Christians. However, please do not think I am recommending Buddhism because it offers a surface peace but rejects God (and Jesus) and therefore can cause people to be separated from God eternally.

We need to train ourselves to "be still and know (relationally) that I am God" (Psalm 46:10) The Hebrew word here for "know" is "yada". It is the same word found in Genesis 4:1: "Adam knew (yada) Eve and she conceived and bore Cain." When we can still our mind and our emotions and allow our human spirit to be more receptive, it is amazing how the Holy Spirit imparts to us out of that intimate relationship. When you are trying to make an important decision, don't try to figure it out in your mind. Your mind will go back and forth weighing the pros and cons. But, if you can just be still and get before the Lord then the Holy Spirit can impart to you what you need to know.

Prayer and Fasting Makes us More Receptive to the Holy Spirit!

I know "fasting" is a bad word in our gluttonous culture, but it helps us to receive from God. We have established that the physical center of the human spirit is the abdomen. What part of your body is not active when you are fasting? The abdomen! Why do I go away and pray and fast? The answer is when I am fasting I become more receptive to the Holy Spirit. The distractions that are always bombarding my mind and emotions fall away. It usually takes me a few hours to get quiet before the Lord, and I often write down all the things I have to do, then I put them aside and forget about them. I am then able to go unencumbered before the Lord soaking in His presence. I may put on some worship music and just lay before the Lord. Sometimes the Holy Spirit will direct me to a passage in the Scripture.

When I was pastoring in Grand Lake, I would walk down to this little waterfall in Rocky Mountain National Park, and I would stay there all day while fasting, I would take my Bible and my Concordance with me and God would just download revelation. My mind and emotions were calm and my abdomen was not working to digest food so I was more receptive to the Holy Spirit. I am sure this principle is taught by other people, but no one ever taught it to me. I learned from experience. This may sound strange to you, but don't throw it out just because it is different. Check the Word. Prayer and fasting empowers us. "And when He (Jesus) had come into the house His disciples asked him privately, 'why could we not cast it out.' So He said to them, "This kind can come out by nothing but prayer and fasting." (Mark 9:28-29).

When we fast and pray and are focused on God, it strengthens us in the Lord. We are less distracted. Fasting does not impress God. You already have God's attention, and He is for you. He so wants to flow through you by the power of the Holy Spirit. It is hard to receive from God when you are emotionally or mentally distracted. Fasting changes us, it doesn't change God. Jesus would periodically go off into the wilderness and pray and fast because He knew how much

He needed to connect with the Father. If Jesus needed to pray and fast at times, maybe it wouldn't hurt us. (Make sure you drink a lot of filtered water. Fasting has great health benefits as well as spiritual benefits.)

When the Holy Spirit's Leading Doesn't Make Sense

There are several examples from Scripture of this principle. Remember Sarah's reaction when she was told that she was going to have a child? She was approaching 90 and laughed out loud at God. Her reasoning said, "No way!" But eventually she and Abraham overcame unbelief and trusted God. Then Isaac, the child of promise, was born miraculously.

How about Mary, the mother of Jesus? Theologians believe she was only about 13 or 14 years old, when she was told about the coming pregnancy. She was engaged at the time and by law, she would be stoned to death if she had sexual relations outside the engagement. The Angel of the Lord came to Mary and told her that she was highly favored, and was going to have a child by the Holy Spirit, and He would be the Messiah. You can imagine what was going through her mind. I'm sure she thought that Joseph would divorce her, and she would be killed or be a laughingstock because she was going to have an illegitimate child. But, she pressed in and told the angel, "Behold the maidservant of the Lord. Let it be to me according to your word." (Luke 1:38) Wow, what faith! Listen to what Mary said: "My soul magnifies the Lord, And my spirit has rejoiced in God my Savior." Mary received this revelation in her human spirit first, then embraced it in her soul even when it didn't make sense.

Then there was Gideon and his army of 32,000. The Israelites were vastly outnumbered by the army of the Amalakites. God told

Gideon to go down to the water and reduce the number of his soldiers to 300. That seemed totally ridiculous, but Gideon obeyed. Remember Gideon was hiding from the Amalakites when God came to him and called him "a mighty man of valor." If he had been victorious in the battle with his 32,000 men, he could have claimed the glory. But the unlikely victory with only 300 men had to be God. So God was praised. Funny how God likes the odds stacked against Him. This is another reason we cannot operate just out of our intellect. When we are trying to make a decision, intellectual reasoning's can often try to negate what God is relaying to us by the Holy Spirit.

I had been out of ministry for about three years. I had run a small Christian High School and later became involved in sales, enjoying both experiences. I went away to pray and fast for a couple of days and the Lord prompted me by saying, "I'm calling you back into pastoring."

"Okay" I said, "but I'm telling no one and sending out no resumes. You are a big God – you'll get me there."

Two months later I got a call from a couple I had ministered with in Haiti. They asked if I would consider coming to their church and trying out for the pastor since theirs had left. I agreed to come. When I got to the church, it was a rundown old warehouse which had been a sheet metal shop. There was a small sanctuary and a couple of small offices. The rest of the building was dirty and dusty. The Lord had told me to preach on hope and when I entered the building I felt heaviness and depression. A lady got up and gave a 15 minute testimony which made no sense. They served communion, but we weren't given any instructions on whether to hold or take the elements.

I said to the Lord "There's no way you're calling me here; I can do a lot better." But that still, small voice said: "No, this is where I am calling you. These are sheep without a shepherd."

Now this went totally against my rational mind. Then I found out they were $50,000 in debt. I thought, "Wow, this doesn't make any sense!" But I obeyed the Lord and am I glad I did. I have been the pastor here at this same church for over 28 years and God has done great things. We built a fantastic facility on 53 acres, and God has blessed us abundantly seeing many transformed lives. I am so glad I obeyed the promptings of the Holy Spirit!

Seeking Clarity

"*We are* destroying sophisticated arguments *and* every exalted and proud thing that sets itself up against the [true] knowledge of God, and *we are* taking every thought *and* purpose captive to the obedience of Christ" (2 Cor. 10:5 AMP). Train yourself to do this over time. When God imparts something to me, I press into Him to discern what He is saying. Sometimes I question if this is God so I ask the Holy Spirit to increase the strength of the impartation if it is Him. My mind often fights me because it may be out of the ordinary. Sometimes it lines up rationally with what I am thinking but often not. I have chosen to be obedient to Him even if I look foolish and it doesn't make sense. I have missed it at times, but I have learned from those experiences and am thankful for His grace.

I remember a few years ago I was ministering at a church in Spokane, Washington. I felt a strong prophetic word for a couple and called them out. I explained I saw that they were trying to make a decision to start a new business and had decided to go ahead, but they were filled with fear. I said "God is calling you to do this – fear not.' They looked ecstatic. Then I added, "You have just come through a major marriage battle..."

When I got to my room that night I asked the Lord how I did. He went back over everything with me but said I should not have added the part about the "marriage battle." "That was not the Holy Spirit," He explained. I suddenly felt terrible and started condemning myself. "Please Lord, let me make this right." I was leaving to go back to Colorado the next day.

That morning the Pastor of the church picked me up for breakfast, and then headed off to the airport. He mentioned he had one quick stop to make. Guess who it was? It was the couple with whom I had blown it. When I saw the couple in their new appliance store, the pastor said, "You were right on last night. This couple is opening a new appliance store. I thought we could pray over them." I was overjoyed and said to them that I had added the part about the marriage struggle. They smiled and said they were so encouraged by the word about their business, they didn't think about the other part. The husband added, "It did puzzle me because we have been getting along very well considering the stress."

I confessed, "Well I just added the last part, it wasn't the Holy Spirit." Then I asked them to forgive me, and they did of course. I felt so much better. I was learning not to embellish what the Holy Spirit brings.

Sometimes He will just give me a picture, let's say of a light bulb. I used to try and figure out what it meant. Now I just relay the picture, and if He doesn't add anything, I don't either! I don't know how many light bulbs failed before Thomas Edison successfully created one that worked. He was asked if he got frustrated at failing over 10,000 times. He said "No" and that he was glad to have discovered 10,000 ways not to make a light bulb bringing him closer to the one that could work. In the same way, the Holy Spirit leads, guides, and directs us. If you miss it, don't feel condemned just learn from it.

Praying in the Spirit Helps us to Receive From the Holy Spirit

It is not wrong to pray out of our intellects. Lots of times we pray for people and situations in this manner. But there is a deeper level of prayer called "praying in the spirit." Ephesians 6 talks about the armor of God. These are our spiritual weapons. We have the "breast-plate of righteousness," we have the "shield of faith" that quench the fiery darts of the enemy, the "helmet of salvation," keeping our minds focused. Also, our "feet are shod with the gospel of peace," keeping our feet safe from injury to bring the good news.

So far it mentions only protective armor. Notice there is no "butt plate of righteousness!" That is because we are supposed to be going forward, not retreating. Notice the armor protects us from frontal attack, but we also have two important offensive weapons. We have the "sword of the Spirit" which is the Word of God which we use to damage the enemy. The word used is "rhema" not "logos". Rhema is revelation knowledge of the word made alive by the Holy Spirit. This we use to damage the enemy. Notice it says "sword of the Spirit" meaning it is the Holy Spirit that makes the word powerful. The other offensive weapon is "praying always in the Spirit." This is a very powerful weapon and I will talk more in depth about praying in the Spirit (which can be in our native language inspired by the Spirit or in "tongues.")

Several years ago at The Rock things were going very well. Unfortunately there was this person who came against me in a very strong way. He was a well respected businessman and head of the board of directors. He accused me of having an affair with his wife, who was my secretary. This was a lie but he was very convincing and had gotten many people to believe him. He wouldn't confront me, but said God would reveal this to all. Suddenly I realized that all the good things that were happening could be destroyed by this lie. I called some people that I trusted to gather in my home for a time of prayer. As we were praying in the Spirit, I had an open vision. (I have only had an open vision three times in my life). This time the board member turned into a needle and began hooking people. Then he turned into a dragon. I could feel the hot breath of the dragon, and I was afraid. I wanted to run! So I stood up and I didn't tell anyone what I was seeing. Suddenly I felt the hand of God (or an angel) on my back, and I experienced peace. The Lord spoke in a non-audible voice, "Speak the Word of God into the dragon's mouth."

I still could feel the hot breath of the dragon, and I still wanted to flee. But I began speaking the word as the Holy Spirit led me: "No weapon formed against me shall prosper and every lying tongue that rises in judgment, we shall condemn." I went on: "Thank you Jesus that you saw Satan fall like lightning from Heaven. You have given us authority to tread on serpents and scorpions and over all the power of the enemy and nothing shall by any means harm us."

As the Word would come to me, I would just speak it out into the dragon's mouth. And as I did this the dragon began to slowly shrink until it eventually evaporated. So, I told the intercessors gathered there what had just happened. Now I had planned in the next couple of days to go to the other board members and convince them that this was a lie. The intercessors all said not to do that because God has shown He was obviously going to take care of the situation. "We just all need to speak the Word into the dragon's mouth." Over the next few days we did this.

Now this prayer meeting happened on a Sunday night, and on Wednesday afternoon the Holy Spirit instructed me to call a meeting of all the board members the next morning. This went against my reasoning because I knew this man had convinced the majority of the board I was having an affair. But I obeyed the Spirit's promptings. I typed out all the accusations and made copies for each member. I knew most of the board members thought that he was telling the truth.

That Thursday morning I was on pins and needles. There was dead silence while they read through the accusations. Suddenly one elder stood up and told the accuser that he had lied, and he needed to ask for forgiveness. Another got up and chastened him. Then another and another did the same. What I didn't know was the Holy Spirit had spoken truth to each individual over the last three days! It came to the light that this greatly respected board member was having an affair with his secretary. He was trying to get rid of his wife and run the church. He had told me several times to keep preaching my great messages and allow the board to run the church. He said that I was a great preacher and should not get bogged down with the day-to-day stuff. That all sounded good to me. Ironically, he had stood up in front of the church a few weeks earlier and said what a great job I was doing and kissed me on the cheek! He failed because God is a great God, and "greater is He who is in us than he who is in the world!"

That sprit-led prayer time using the Sword of the Spirit was instrumental in foiling the enemy attack. When we use the Word of God by the Spirit it is very powerful. I had felt a tremendous anointing from God in the midst of this warfare. Although I had been very anxious and worried, the anxiety fled. When you really get below the emotions and intellect and get down into your human spirit the Holy Spirit can do the miraculous. Romans 8:26 NLT says: *"And the Holy Spirit helps us in our weakness. For example, we don't know what God wants us to pray for. But the Holy Spirit prays for us with groaning that cannot be expressed in words..."* Groaning comes from the center of your human spirit and not from your intellect. Groanings originate in the abdomen and in this case were Spirit led. *"And the Father who knows all hearts knows what the Spirit is saying, for the Spirit pleads for us believers in harmony with God's own will."* (v.27) The literal meaning from the Greek is that "The Holy Spirit comes and takes hold together with us and prays with groanings that cannot be uttered in articulate native language." The Holy Spirit comes and prays with us at a much deeper and effective manner beyond our intellect.

On the Brink of Death

A few years ago I got a call from a husband in our church who said that his wife was in surgery, and that she was dying. He was crying on the phone, and I could feel his desperation. We had a little prayer room in the front of the house, and I went in and prayed. The Holy Spirit prompted me to come against the "spirit of death" that was trying to take her out. She was only in her late twenties with three children. He told me I needed to go to the hospital immediately. I called a guy en route who was a friend of theirs, and I picked him up. We were praying in the Spirit (with "groanings.") We were praying in English and in tongues and in every way we could. We were crying out to God because we knew this was a very serious situation. As I was driving up I-25 right where it crosses I-470, I felt a release and peace internally. I said to the guy with me that she was going to be okay. There was a heaviness that broke in my sprit, and I just knew beyond a doubt that she was going to be okay.

We got to the hospital in about 15 minutes, and we went in. About 15 minutes after we had arrived, the surgeon comes out with his surgical mask hanging around his neck and says, "About 30 minutes ago, we found where she was bleeding and we were able to stop it. She is going to be fine!" What a relief to her husband, the kids and the relatives gathered there. Her heartbeat had dropped dangerously low, and she had lost a lot of blood. She had been on the brink of death.

Usually, you don't know what effect you are having; you just pray in faith. But I remember that night that there was such a depth of prayer that I know we made a significant difference. Because of the exact timing I got to see the difference that it made. I am not taking credit for what God had done for He brought the healing. But I know their friend and I contributed powerfully to what God wanted to accomplish. You never know how powerful your prayers are when you cooperate with the Holy Spirit.

Did you know Jesus groaned two times before he raised Lazarus from the dead? Mary and Martha's brother, Lazarus, had died. He had been dead for four days. All hope seemed gone. Jesus had not come when Mary asked, and I think Mary was a little ticked off at him. "Therefore, when Jesus saw her weeping, and several Jews weeping with her, He groaned in the spirit and was troubled. And He said, 'Where have you laid him?' (John 11:32) Continue further, "Then Jesus, again groaning in Himself, came to the tomb." (v. 38).

Up against an extremely difficult situation, Jesus resorts to groaning in the spirit which was the Holy Spirit teaming with Him with groaning through his human spirit. When He told them to take the stone away from the tomb, Martha said it was going to stink because he had been dead for four days (Martha was always practical). But Jesus ignored her and said: "Lazarus, come forth." And, Lazarus came forth risen from the dead! Yes Lazarus' grave clothes stunk, but he was alive and well!

What About Praying For People To Get Saved?

Charles Finney had one of the greatest retention rates in revival. When people gave their life to Christ, about 85% of them continued to follow and grow in the Lord. In revivals today, it is usually under 10% who continue to follow Christ. Finney would send Father Nash with his intercession team into a city days before he would come to do a revival meeting. They would rent rooms in a hotel and pray and fast confining themselves for several days before Finney would come into town.

In Rochester, New York before a series of life changing revival meetings, the hotel manager called an ambulance because he thought someone was dying in the room where they were praying. They were groaning in the Spirit in deep intercessory prayer and the poor manager became frightened. This type of intercessory prayer would break strongholds over the city so when Charles Finney would arrive, people would fall on the ground under deep conviction crying out for salvation even before he had gotten up to preach. These prayer warriors had broken the strongholds of the enemy through praying in the Spirit. (Jude 20)

The Holy Spirit is your ally. He is your direct link to the Father's desires for you. He is your advocate before the throne. He is your teacher and your guide. He even intercedes on your behalf (Romans 8:26). He is not "spooky" or "weird." He wants to be in close fellowship with you at all times. I encourage you to lean into Him, to explore the depths of what He has for you, and to experiment with listening to Him, praying with Him, and acting on what you hear.

Let's go farther and find out how the Holy Spirit builds you up and keeps you wrapped in the love of God.

Chapter 13:

The Power of Love

When you pray in the Spirit, you are not only building yourself up in faith but also keeping yourself in the love of God! "But you, beloved, building yourselves up on your most holy faith, praying in the Holy Spirit. Keep yourselves in the love of God, looking for the mercy of our Lord Jesus Christ unto eternal life." ((Jude 20-21)) The Gospels reveal that Jesus was often "moved with compassion" before working a miracle. He felt and showed incredible love. When He acted, the motivation was love and the impact was great. Love is so powerful. After the Apostle Paul talks about the gifts of the spirit, he emphasizes that these gifts work best when motivated by love. (1 Corinthians 12:13) Love is the key.

Recently, I was leaving the hospital in Castle Rock when I was drawn to a young man sitting by the entrance. As I approached him, I felt this overwhelming compassion. As I got closer, I saw he was crying. I sat beside him and put my arm around him. He then put his arm around me, and I realized he smelled strongly of B.O. and alcohol. Judgment began to rise up in me, but fortunately God's compassion was greater. As I listened through the ears of love, this man proceeded to tell me he lost his father, mother and sister to cancer in the last three months.

"I've lost everything" he said, now sobbing uncontrollably.

"May I pray for you?" "yes," he replied.

After I prayed, he thanked me for a great prayer and then said "I'm a f…ing Christian."

My heart went out to him as I explained when we go through such losses we feel like f…ing Christians. I felt tremendous compassion, as we talked awhile. After some time I asked, "Is there anything more I can do for you?"

"No," he said, "you've already done so much. Thank you, I'll never forget this moment. I know God cares about me now."

Amazing what His love can do!

Love opens doors that no man can open or close! Each year I travel to Pakistan with Leif Hetland. He has built very strong relationships through love with key Muslim leaders. He has flown them to his home in Atlanta and helped them financially and through prayer. He is known as the "Apostle of Love" in Pakistan. Before we were conducting open air meetings two of these very influential Muslim Imams would tell the crowds to listen to this man. Then they would leave and Leif would preach the Gospel with great compassion. Two years ago we saw 87,000 Muslims respond positively to the Gospel. We also saw many miracles and healings. Love opens doors that no man can open or close!

Love Comes Through Big Time

In 1982 I went with a group of pastors and leaders on my first mission trip to the island of Haiti. This was (and still is) the poorest country in the Western Hemisphere. We went in August, and it was so hot and humid…a far cry from Colorado! We held some crusades in Port-au-Prince, but then we broke up into groups of three or four people. We were assigned to small churches out in the country where there was even greater poverty. I went with a translator and two ladies to a tin roofed shack. The floors were dirt and smelled like urine. There were no walls just posts holding up the roof.

I preached through the translator, gave people a chance to receive Christ, and invited people forward if they wanted prayer. After praying for a few people, a large lady with sweat pouring down her face came forward with a tiny baby in her arms. The baby had mucus running from its nose, and its eyes were filled with puss. I figured the infant to be only days old. When the mother placed the crying baby in my hands, I was shocked how the infant seemed to be on fire, she was so hot. Suddenly, I felt this overwhelming surge of compassion for this poor little baby. This feeling of love was almost incapacitating. I also felt so inadequate and too weak to be able to help. If the baby didn't get healed, I couldn't say, "Take it to a nearby clinic for treatment." There was nothing like that within miles.

In my desperation, still feeling this incredible compassion and helplessness for the baby, I lifted my eyes toward Heaven and cried to the Lord, "Heal this child in Jesus' name."

As I brought the baby down, it seemed she had cooled in my hands. But then I thought to myself: "*You want the baby healed so badly that you are imagining this*." I knew when I placed the infant back in the mother's hands, she would know.

When I gave back her child, she started screaming so loud. She was shouting something in a language I didn't understand. The interpreter told me she was shouting, "Thank you Jesus, you healed my baby!" over and over. I will never forget that night. When I got back to the compound where we were staying, I was overwhelmed with emotion. I had never felt that kind of love for anyone before. His love goes beyond measure!

Paul talked about how love motivated him and compelled him beyond anything else (see 2 Cor. 5:14). The deep love that drove Paul is the same love that needs to motivate us. When you really love somebody, you are not going to be worried about your reputation or what they think of you. You are not even going to be worried about how people respond to you. At times when I have had an anointing to break demonic oppression off of someone, it can look weird and some have accused me of putting on a show. This really hurts, but I can't let that stop me because people have told me how much it helps them. Love will cause us to care more about helping the person than our reputation. If you are too concerned about what people think, you will not be obedient to the leading of the Holy Spirit, and you will not fulfill the destiny God has for your life.

Balancing Truth And Love

Paul talks about the importance of "speaking the truth in love" (Eph 5:15). Ironically, I think my generation is big on truth and sometimes short on love. I've talked with people who want nothing to do with Christianity because they were hammered legalistically with truth and very little love.

On the other hand the younger generation seems to be big on love and short on truth. One well known pastor said that because he grew up in an unloving, legalistic church, he saw God as harsh and condemning. From that vantage point, he preached a strong false doctrine that there was no Hell, because God is so loving He would never send anyone to Hell. Everyone eventually goes to Heaven.

The truth is that God doesn't send anyone to Hell, although some will go there (see 2 Pet. 3:9). In fact Hell was created for the fallen angels. However, Jesus talked about Hell as a reality and He wasn't making it up. He died for everyone's sin, but rejection of Jesus Christ will keep a person from Heaven. God wanted everyone to avoid Hell; that's why He sent Jesus Christ to earth to give His life. "For God so loved the world that He gave His only begotten Son, that whoever believes in Him should not perish but have everlasting life." (John 3:16)

We need to show love, but not be afraid to speak truth in love. God's word is truth (John 8:31-32). If we really love someone, we will care enough to bring truth, but only in love. When the woman caught in adultery was brought to Jesus, He spent a lot of time showing her His love and grace. He bent down and wrote in the dirt telling those without sin to cast the first stone. (Under the law a woman caught in adultery was to be stoned to death.) Then as the crowd drops their stones and backs away, He asks the woman what happened to her accusers? Then He speaks powerful words: "Neither do I condemn you." The woman is now blown away by His love. But Jesus didn't stop there, demonstrating only mercy. He went on to say lovingly to this woman, "Go and sin no more." If Jesus had said "I don't condemn you-whatever." That would not have been love. Love speaks truth which is spoken out of the platform of love.

A few years ago there was a lady living a lesbian life style who lived across from us. I really enjoyed talking with her and would make an effort to reach out since the rest of the neighborhood seemed to shun her. One day I saw a U Haul in her driveway, and I walked over offering my services since she was moving out of town.

After working up a sweat, she asked me "Why are you being nice to me? I know you are head pastor of The Rock Church."

I answered, "Well you are my neighbor and I love you."

She thanked me so much for helping her, and then asked honestly: "You know I'm a lesbian. What does God think of that and what does the Bible say?"

I was set back. We had a great relationship, and I was tempted to say, "Oh, God loves you no matter how you live." That would have been partial truth, but would not have been the whole truth. I told her that the Bible condemns homosexuality as sin along with heterosexual sin and other areas as well. Then I shared how Jesus died for all our sins both large and small. I encouraged her to put her trust in Jesus and let Him work it out. She thanked me for my honesty. With tears in both our eyes we hugged, and she drove off. Sometimes it is hard to speak the truth even in love!

The love of God is poured out into our hearts by the Holy Spirit (Rom. 5:5). He gives us love beyond anything we can comprehend. When I am literally moved by His love while praying, it seems like there are much greater results. Be open, not only to the things of the Spirit but allow His love to be the motivating force in your life.

Be Led by the Spirit

The good news is that we get to be led by the Spirit, and we get to impact people's lives. Sometimes it may be a person at work who you sense is going through something emotionally. You may put your arm around them and offer to pray for them in a non-weird way. You can't believe how that impacts a person's life. People don't care how much you know until they know how much your care. Don't let fear of how you will be received or what they will think of you keep you from acting out of love. We need to risk. If we are unwilling to fail, we will never succeed!

Peter failed miserably by denying Jesus three times, yet he got to preach on the Day of Pentecost where 3,000 plus people came into the Kingdom! Peter was a risk taker and demonstrated this when he jumped out of the boat and walked on water before sinking. God earnestly desires us to be led by His Spirit.

I pray that you and I would be led by the Spirit daily. To be honest sometimes I know I am being led by the Holy Spirit, but other times I am led by my own feelings. Sometimes I get distracted. We need to cut ourselves some slack. We are all human, we're not perfect, but we are growing. As we learn how to walk in the Spirit, He helps us, He guides us, He is with us. He is in us! He loves us even when we fail while trying to obey!

A Prayer

"Father, I thank You for each and every person, and I pray that we will all be led by Your Spirit on a daily, moment-by-moment basis. Thank you that you are available to us 24/7. You never leave us. You never forsake us. Help us, Father, to make a difference in this world. Help us to make a difference in the lives of others and let Your love consume us and move us beyond our comfort zones. In Jesus' name, amen."

Section 6

HEALING OF THE BODY

"Christ is the Good Physician. There is no disease He cannot heal; no sin He cannot remove; no trouble He cannot help. He is the Balm of Gilead, the Great Physician!
- Amy Carmichael

Physical disease and pain can drastically inhibit the believer's attempt to serve God. The Bible says Jesus took "stripes" on His back for our healing. Does God want to bring healing to us or are we to accept our disease as God's will? In this section we will explore the answers to these important questions and examine what role the Holy Spirit plays.

Chapter 14:

Does God Still Heal?

Impacted by a Church Growth Conference

I was attending a Church Growth Conference several years ago. The main speaker, a pastor of a mega church of about 10,000 people, said: "If you want to grow a big church you must avoid several things. First, don't preach on healing because people will leave your church when they don't get healed. Don't get into prophesy because you will draw 'weirdos' who will drive others away. Stay away from deliverance in any form because it will stir up the demonic and make people uncomfortable. And whatever you do, avoid talking about the gifts of the Spirit and especially "speaking in tongues." This will send people headed for the exits by the droves." He went on to say, "It's okay to talk about the Holy Spirit but in generalities."

He continued to explain how he was Spirit-filled and believed in all those things, but not for growing a big church. He gave statistics and was the picture of confidence and success in the American Church, so his words had a strong impact on me.

Over the next couple of years I began to pull back from the things of the Spirit. I subtly stopped emphasizing healing, prophecy and deliverance. And I vowed to myself not to bring up the controversial subject of "speaking in tongues" except in private meetings. He had also mentioned keeping flags and dancing out of the services. "These make new people or unbelievers very uncomfortable," he said. So I began to move toward a more "seeker sensitive" model, fearing I would drive people away. "Don't talk about the devil," he had said, "just emphasize the positive!" This all seemed to make sense, and during this time our church did grow, but I was restless in my spirit. Then a few years ago God really began to deal with my heart and my motives. "Are you trying to build a large, shallow pond to make yourself look successful, or are you building my Kingdom?" To be honest I was attempting to increase the numbers so I could feel accomplished. It was all about me. How sad.

Convicted, I went away and prayed and fasted for a few days. During that time I became aware of selfish ambition and fear of man in my heart which both saddened and sickened me. How could I have gone this far off track from what God wanted for me? He reminded me about my days as a pastor in Grand Lake where the Holy Spirit was free to move. We had experienced a mini-revival where people were saved, healed and delivered on a weekly basis. God was moving and the presence of the Holy Spirit was so strong that people would drive all the way from Denver to be there. Oh, it got messy at times and some who were uncomfortable left, but it was fun and fulfilling. Our little church was running over 300 on Sunday morning in a town with a population of 500. But more importantly people's lives were being transformed.

Jesus encountered me and asked me, "What kind of disciples would I have produced had I followed that mega church pastor's formula? I might have had more disciples and bigger crowds, but could they have changed the world after I had gone to be with my Father?"

Suddenly, I had a whole different perspective on success. To be successful in the Kingdom, Jesus was telling me that I needed to be obedient to Him and true to who He had created me to be and do. Wow! To produce the kind of disciples He produced was what He wanted for our church. What a turning point in my life.

Rather than scaring everybody by proclaiming we were now going to go after healing, prophecy, deliverance, tongues, and the gifts of the Spirit, I just began to slowly embrace the areas I had subtly turned away from. I began bringing them into my messages. We started healing rooms and began to train many more altar ministers, and prophetic teams. We really started going after the presence of God and before every service back in our prayer room we prayed for people to have an encounter with Jesus.

Miracles Still Happen!

About this time an incredible miracle happened at our church. A lady named Rae had come to our church broken emotionally. Her 21 year old son had been murdered and her husband had a heart attack. Her daughter had a nervous breakdown and then as if that weren't enough, her husband lost his job and had been unemployed for 3 years. To compound the problems she had been diagnosed with Primary, Progressive MS (Multiple Sclerosis). She would come forward for prayer with her walker or cane but was often bedridden. Talk about down and out! Yet God came through miraculously. Just before an evening service a lady in the prayer room spoke healing over her. She first began to walk and then run! Two weeks later she was able to walk down the aisle at her daughter's wedding and dance with her husband at the reception. He got a new job, and they both became so excited about Jesus. Today Rae is the pastor over prayer, altar ministry and prophetic teams at our church. Talk about a transformed life! Yes, "Jesus is the same yesterday, today and forever!" (Heb. 13:8)

It was exciting as the shift began. Some were ecstatic while others left the church (just like that mega church pastor warned). We had a couple with whom we were very close. We had vacationed in Mexico with them and really enjoyed their friendship. They came to me and my wife Yvonne to tell us why they were leaving the church. They explained that there was too much emphasis on healing and the Holy Spirit. "We don't like that so we are leaving," they said.

I would like to tell you that their response didn't bother me, but it did. It really hurt, and I wondered if maybe I was putting too much emphasis on the things of the Spirit. When I would take this concern to the Lord, He would encourage me, telling me He also had followers leave Him and that I should keep sharing in these areas. Sometimes there is a price to pay when you choose to please Jesus and not people. Paul writes: "Obviously, I'm not trying to win the approval of people, but of God. If pleasing people were my goal, I would not be Christ's servant." (Gal 1:10 NLT)

Once I had chosen to be obedient, we saw many miraculous healings from all different types of cancer to various sicknesses. We have since trained children as well as adults to pray for healing. One Sunday morning we brought the children into the main service to pray with the altar ministers for those who were sick. Here is the testimony from a man in our congregation.

> "On September 18th 1996, I was involved in a pretty bad helicopter accident involving me and a 22,500 lb

Blackhawk helicopter. To make a long story short, I ended up being crushed from my waist down. I suffered a dislocated right hip, a crushed right femur and two blown out knees. Anyway, I was left in traction for 4 days and self-administered morphine before the docs decided what to do.

That following Monday, a Chaplain came into my room and gave me last rights and wished me luck. I had surgery and they put a titanium rod in my leg to help the bone heal. My surgeon (a Colonel) told me I would never walk again and should consider the 100% disability medical discharge. I was 21 at the time and felt indestructible, even though I was considered a lost cause. I taught myself to walk again, with the help of a walker, then crutches, then with nothing. God was carrying me. I was running, taking PT tests and almost as fit as I was before the accident. I began flying again 6 months after I was discharged from the hospital. I ended my career as an instructor pilot for the same helicopter that almost took my life. But for over 20 years I have been dealing with the horrible pain from that day.

In a service when Pastor Curt was reading off words of knowledge that the children had received, I felt a tug at my heart to go up and get prayed for. Caleb had gotten the word: a military person who was hurt in the service. He prayed, and I prayed in agreement. When he was done, I promise you as sure as I'm breathing, the pain was gone! I have not slowed down and have continued to work as hard as I ever and have not had an ounce of pain. I want to publicly confess this testimony and thank Caleb and to encourage him for his awesome God given gift to me."

- Shawn Ferris

Physical Healing For Today?

There are many types of healing from physical to emotional. I believe God cares about our whole being: our human spirit, our soul (mind, emotions, and will) and our physical bodies. "Dear friend, I hope all is well with you and that you are as healthy in body as you are strong in spirit" (3 John 2 NLT).

I mentioned in the opening of this book that I actually died when I was 4 ½ years old. Though Jesus raised me back from the dead, I wasn't healed of asthma in that moment. I missed more school than I attended in kindergarten, first, and second grade. I was sick all the time and I hated it. In fact, my parents would make me take a nap in the afternoon when all the other kids would be outside playing football or baseball.

Going forward, that asthma stayed with me. I remember coming out of football games in High School and grabbing my asthma inhaler and taking a hit and then going back into the game. Even in wrestling meets I would hit the inhale sometimes before a match.

A few months after I got saved, I went to a service where a man was teaching on healing and then laying hands on the sick. I went forward and got miraculously healed of asthma. I never had another attack. For those of you that have asthma or COPD, you know how scary it is when you can't get your breath. I give God the glory for that healing. We continue to see the conditions of asthma and COPD healed during our services in our healing rooms!

In that same service our son, Mike, got healed. When he was less than one year old, he was extremely pigeon toed. Doctors said he would need to have surgery and after that he would have to have casts. You can imagine how hard that would be on a toddler, so we prayed fervently. The doctor said "I can't believe it, but no surgery or casts will be necessary." I was deeply moved by my son's healing when he was 14 months old.

I learned God was a healer even early in my Christian walk. And yet, some of the churches I attended never talked about healing. Some actually said that healing and miracles were not for today. Recently I talked to a friend of mine who is a pastor of a large church and I asked him, "Do you guys ever talk about healing and pray for the sick?"

He said, "No I don't talk about healing, and we don't pray for healing because if somebody did not get healed, they would get disappointed and maybe leave our church or even turn away from God. Plus I think healing passed away and is not for today."

Wow, I thought to myself, this is really sad! Healing is part of the Gospel. When Jesus first sent out the disciples, He told them, "And as you go, preach, saying, 'The kingdom of heaven is at hand.' Heal the sick, cleanse the lepers, raise the dead, cast out demons. Freely you have received, freely give" (Matt. 10:7-8).

Is It His Will?

A question that people often have is this: "Is it God's will to physically heal or does He sometimes bring sickness or allow it in order to develop character?" There is no doubt that our character can develop through trials, struggles and even physical illness. The

Apostle Paul wrote: "And not only that, but we also glory in tribulations, knowing that tribulation produces perseverance; and perseverance, character; and character, hope"… (Rom. 5:3-4) Does God bring on the sickness to develop character? The answer is a resounding "No!" Jesus never told a sick person: "Go your way my Father has made you sick so you could develop stronger character." No, Jesus healed all types of sickness and disease. He was manifesting God's will. If you put some horrible sickness on your children to teach them a lesson, you could be arrested for child abuse. I want to tell you that God is a loving, healing God, not a child abuser.

Some people believe that while God has the power to heal, it may not be His will to heal. When I first came to Castle Rock, I was having breakfast with a pastor. I suggested that we should pray for each other. He asked how he could pray for me. I told him that I was fighting a head cold, and I had not slept well the night before and that I was congested. "Please pray for me" I said, "because I need to get over this quickly as I have a busy week."

He prayed: "Heavenly Father, I have never seen anybody healed, I am not sure you even heal or if it is your will, but if you can touch J.R., please do." I will tell you I felt worse *after* his prayer than before! It is important to know where God stands in the area of healing. He has the power to heal and it is His will that you should be whole.

When Jesus came to earth, He came to demonstrate the will of the Father. He said to Phillip, "If you have seen Me, you have seen the Father" (John 14:9). There was a man who came to Jesus and said, "Jesus, I know you <u>can</u> heal, (you have the power to heal), but <u>is it your will</u>? Will you heal me?"

Let's pick up the story in Luke 5:12-13 "In one of the villages, Jesus met a man with an advanced case of leprosy…" Now before I go any further, let me explain about leprosy. In our day and age, we have cancer, we have other things that are really bad, but leprosy was a disease which distorted the face and turned limbs into nubs. If a person had leprosy they were isolated or put with other lepers. They were total outcasts. Doomed.

The man who came to Jesus had an advanced case of leprosy. He bowed his face to Jesus, begging to be healed. "Lord", he said "if you are willing you can make me clean." In other words if it is your will, I know you can heal me and make me clean. Notice he said "I know you have the power to heal me, but is it your will?" A lot of Christians and non believers have that same question today. Jesus reached out and touched him and said, "I am willing (it is My will). Be healed." Instantly, the leprosy disappeared. Jesus instructed him not to tell anyone but to go to the priest and get checked out to make sure he got a clean bill of health. Following the example of Jesus, we believe it is important to confirm healings medically. Even though someone feels or thinks they are healed, we want them to go get it checked out with a doctor. Then come back to us and let us know it is a verified healing. We don't want to make a big issue out of it unless it is a verified healing.

In the Lord's Prayer Jesus told us to pray, "Your will be done on earth as it is in Heaven." Is there any sickness or disease in Heaven? The way you know if something is God's perfect will is to look at Heaven and look at the Garden of Eden. For now we live in between. We live in a fallen world so there is sickness and disease in our world. God is a loving God; He never puts sickness and disease on people. He is a lover. We know He is not the author of sickness and disease, because Satan is the author of illness (although not all diseases are directly tied to him). However, indirectly he is the author of all sickness and disease. He brought it on the earth when Adam and Eve sinned in the Garden of Eden. "The thief does not come except to steal, and to kill, and to destroy. I have come that they may have life, and that they may have *it* more abundantly" (John 10:10).

When we understand this truth, we can pray powerfully for God's will for people to be healed. We can rebuke and curse sickness and release God's healing in Jesus Name! God is such a good God that He will take difficulties, even tragedies, and bring good out of them. Sometimes when people go through physical illness, their attitude and heart change for the better. Unfortunately, sometimes these same people will say that God put the sickness on them so they would be a better person. No, God is a good God: "And we know that God causes everything to work together for the good of those who love God and are called according to His purpose for them" (Rom. 8:28 NLT).

When God takes a difficult situation and brings good out of it, that doesn't mean God was the initiator of that difficulty. It is hard to go to God to receive healing if you think He is the author of your disease. If He caused the sickness then going to the doctor or taking medicine would be going against His will. God uses doctors to perform His will. It is God's will that you be healed. Going to a doctor is not a lack of faith, it is exercising good stewardship over your body and your health. Doctors can work with God to help bring healing.

Chapter 15:

Old Covenant or New?

Which is better, the Old Covenant or the New Covenant? "But now Jesus, our High Priest, has been given a ministry that is **far superior to the old** priesthood, for He is the one who mediates for us **a far better covenant with God, based on better promises**" (Heb. 8:6, NLT, emphasis mine). The Old Covenant is a foundation for the New Covenant. So does that mean healing is part of the Old Covenant? Yes. Healing is found in several places in the Old Testament. One of God's names is "Jehovah Rapha" which literally means "the God who heals us" (Ex. 16:26).

It is God's nature to heal. He is a healing God. He wants to make us whole in all ways: spiritually, emotionally, and physically. "Worship the Lord your God and his blessing will be on your food and water. **I will take away sickness from among you**." (Ex. 23:25, emphasis mine)

Psalm 105:37 actually says "there were no sick among them." In other words, when the children of Israel were coming through the wilderness, everyone walked in divine health. God kept over one million Jews healthy–not an easy task. The Psalmist describes God as the one "who forgives all your sins and **heals all your diseases**" (Psalms 103:3 NIV, emphasis mine). The enemy doesn't like this information to get out, because he wants to keep us ignorant. He likes to keep people from receiving everything God has for them.

Physical Healing in the Atonement

When Jesus hung on the cross, He took all the sins of the world upon Himself. As He did that, He literally broke the power of sin and death and hell over everyone. However, a person needs to receive Jesus as their personal Lord and Savior for the forgiveness of their sin for this to become a reality in their life.

The Gospel is not just pie in the sky, by and by, when we die. Now, I am thankful for that, and I am looking forward to Heaven, where we will be with Him. All those old athletic injuries will be gone, and we will get new bodies, and I am going to receive a full head of hair! Isaiah prophesied that the Messiah (Jesus) would take our sickness and disease upon himself as well as our sins and iniquities in the atonement (Isa. 53). This prophecy is quoted by Peter in the New Testament: "He Himself bore our sins in His body on the cross..." (which is again the atonement) "so that we might die to sins and live for righteousness...by whose stripes you were healed." (I Pet. 2:24)

Do you remember Jesus took 39 lashes which literally ripped the flesh off His back before He went to the cross? That was part of the atonement. Not only did He die for our sins, He also purchased our healing when He took the stripes on His back. When you begin to understand that, you can walk in the fullness of what God has accomplished: 2,000 years ago healing became a greater reality through Jesus. You were healed 2,000 years ago, so receive it, because you can't earn it. You can exercise, eat healthy, and take care of yourself making sure you get enough rest. This is wise stewardship and will contribute to your health but you cannot earn healing.

In the Old Covenant, healing resulted from obedience. In fact, Deuteronomy says if you act according to God's will, if you obey the law, then you will be blessed in every way. Your body, your barns and fields will be blessed. You will be blessed wherever you go (Deut. 28).

Further on in this chapter, there is a long list of curses that will come out of disobedience. This was called the "curse of the law." Thank God we are now under grace. We are free to make bad decisions but bad decisions result in bad consequences. Grace does not necessarily free us from consequences but should empower us to want to obey from the heart and receive forgiveness when we blow it.

The scripture says it this way: "If you sow to the flesh you are going to reap to the flesh. If you sow to the Spirit, you are going to reap to the Spirit." (Gal 6:7-8) When we mess up, there are still ramifications for it. We are under grace because Jesus broke the curse of the law and can alter and lessen the consequences. The consequences are not God punishing us. He placed His wrath on Jesus at the cross. Jesus freed us by His grace: "Christ redeemed us from the curse of the law by becoming a curse for us, for it is written: 'Cursed is everyone who is hung on a pole.' He redeemed us in order that the blessing given to Abraham might come to the Gentiles through Christ Jesus, so that by faith we might receive the promise of the Spirit." (Gal. 3:13-14 NIV)

I am a Gentile so I am very grateful that Jesus broke the curse of the law over me so that I could receive the blessings of Abraham. As believers these blessings can come upon us, plus we have the promise of the Holy Spirit to come and live in us because of what Jesus has done. I am so grateful to be living in a New Covenant reality!

If it is God's Will to Heal, Why do Some People not Get Healed?

This is an honest and important question. It's true, not everyone gets healed. I remember when I first came to Castle Rock. I did a healing service on a Sunday night, and there was a neighbor who lived about three doors down from us. She had terminal cancer and was given about six to eight weeks to live. Another lady in our church also had terminal cancer with about the same amount of time to live. I prayed for both of them. My neighbor was miraculously healed. She came and knocked on our door. She had gone to the doctor, and they could not find any cancer. She knew she had been miraculously healed. She didn't even go to our church but sadly, the other lady (our member) died a few weeks later. I had prayed for her healing, but now I did her funeral.

This is difficult to comprehend. I don't know why some people get healed while others don't. Some people may say "Well obviously she didn't have enough faith. That is why she didn't get healed." Poppycock! Never, ever say that. You know why? First, you don't know. Second, it crushes the little bit of faith that they may have. If anything, you need to build their faith. You need to speak the Word and let them know that healing is in the atonement and often it is gradual not instantaneous. Let them know God cares for them and loves them. Build up their faith. "Faith works by love" (Gal. 5:6). The word "works" in the Greek is "energeo" which means faith is energized by love not condemnation.

Don't get me wrong, faith is very important. There were times Jesus said after a healing, "Your faith has made you whole." Jesus said we only need to have as much faith as a mustard seed! If I showed you a mustard seed in my hand right now, you could barely see it because it is so little. Jesus never said to someone, "Go, your lack of faith has caused you to be sick." He told some people their faith had made them well, but He never condemned. We always need to love people and build them up.

Sometimes healing happens gradually, and sometimes not at all. I remember during our son Mike's senior year in high school, he was wrestling in the semi-finals of the state tournament, and he got a bad hip pointer. (Just a few weeks earlier he had gradually been healed miraculously of a tear to his rotator cuff). I even went out on the mat to pray for him as the trainer worked on him, but this time he didn't get healed. Even though way ahead in the match, he was disqualified because of the injury and was not able to go into the finals. I don't know why some healing happens dramatically and some healing doesn't happen at all. When we get to Heaven, we will gain His eternal perspective and won't be troubled by this at all. For now we just need to trust that God has the power to heal and it is His desire for us to be healed.

I have seen so many healings in my own life. I remember during a worship service years ago, I was dramatically healed from a neck injury (and surgery) I had sustained in college wrestling during my senior year. This just happened in the worship service- no one even layed hands on me. It was like a chiropractic adjustment from Heaven.

I tore my rotator cuff in my senior year in college, and I never got it fixed. I was roughhousing with my son-in- law about 3 years ago, and I tore it even more. I had to go to the doctor even though I had powerful people like Bill Johnson, Randy Clark (and others) pray for me, but I didn't get healed. Thank God for the surgeon because my shoulder works fine now.

Removing Blocks to Healing

Lack of faith can hinder healing and miracles. In fact in the town of Nazareth where Jesus grew up, he could do no miracles. They mocked him saying that this was Joseph's and Mary's boy, the carpenter. They questioned his messianic call. Mark tells us that Jesus couldn't do any miracles however, a few still got healed. He writes: "He (Jesus) was amazed at their lack of faith" (Mark 6:6 NIV). If you don't believe in healing or you believe God no longer heals today, this can be a block to your healing.

Other believers can come around someone who needs healing and encourage and pray with them. This increases faith. What about the man who was paralyzed? He had four friends who tore a hole in the roof and lowered him down on a litter to Jesus. When Jesus saw their faith He forgave this man's sin and healed him of paralysis (Matt. 9:2). Sometimes it helps to have friends who love you enough to push through the block (like these men did) to acquire your healing.

Don't let your fear of not having enough faith keep you from going after healing. There are times when I have seen healings when I had no or very little faith. Paul wrote to Timothy: "If we are faithless, He remains faithful; He cannot deny Himself." (2 Tim. 2:13) This verse does not encourage you to be faithless. Build a strong relationship with Him; get into His word and spend time in worship. All this helps tremendously to build your faith. His presence gives perspective! It is important to pray with others. There is something powerful about collective faith.

Faith has a lot to do with healing, but let me share a story where I had very little faith for a person I was asked to pray for. I remember one weekend when a lady who attended our church told me her husband was dying of a lung disease. She explained he had worked for several years with highly toxic chemicals. By breathing these the lining of his lungs had been destroyed and his oxygen level was so low, he was dying. The doctors gave him no hope since they could not restore the lining of his lungs. He was on oxygen, but was only given a few more days to live.

Given his hopeless circumstances, I had no faith for this man's healing, but said I would pray for him if they came to the service. She brought him to the service on Sunday. He could hardly walk, even with a walker. At the end of the service she brought him forward for prayer. I laid my hands on his chest and began to pray for a creative miracle. Suddenly I felt hands on top of my hands. I was afraid to open my eyes, but in the Spirit I could see these were Jesus' hands. My faith which had been very low leapt to new heights. I knew beyond any doubt he would be healed, not because of my faith, but because of Jesus!

The next day his wife called me and said when he went back to the hospital, he was able to breathe without oxygen! Monday morning when the doctor came in and examined him, he said, "Something has dramatically changed." His oxygen level was normal. They ran several tests that morning, and released him to go home that afternoon. The doctor shook his head and said "I've never seen anything like this before." This man was totally healed. The next Sunday he came to the service with normal strength and gladly shared his testimony. Wow, is God good or what!

We want to remove all blocks. When I was pastoring up in the mountains, I got to know a pastor of a large church in Denver. He was diagnosed with a brain tumor, so I went down to pray for him. I really liked the guy. He told me I was wasting my time praying for him because he believed it was his "thorn in the flesh." "After all," he told me, "Paul had his thorn in the flesh. I believe this brain tumor is my thorn in the flesh, and I believe God is going to take me to Heaven because of this."

I said, "No, that is a misinterpretation of 'thorn in the flesh,' and I went on to explain what the thorn in the flesh was. Some theologians say this thorn in the flesh was that Paul had runny eyes or some disease that God wouldn't heal him from. So they imply God basically said, "Suck it up, Paul. Just learn to live with it."

Let's look more closely at the passage: "or because of these surpassingly great revelations. Therefore, in order to keep me from becoming conceited, I was given a thorn in my flesh..." (2 Cor. 12:7-9 NIV). Paul had a lot of revelation. He wrote much of the revelation knowledge of the New Testament. He went to the third Heaven and even talked about it. I mean, he had incredible revelation! Paul felt that this "thorn in the flesh" kept him from getting puffed up or conceited. He believed that this humbled him. Paul defines the "thorn in the flesh," Saying: "A thorn in the flesh, was given to me, **a** messenger of Satan, to torment me**."** Did it come from God? No way. It was a messenger of Satan. The word "messenger" in the original Greek is "*angelos*." This can also be translated "angel." A fallen angel came against him and demonically attacked him.

God didn't just tell Paul he was going to have to live with it, but said, 'My grace is sufficient for you" 'My grace is sufficient for you" (2 Cor. 12:8). Notice God wasn't saying that Paul was just going to have to live with it. No, He tells him: "My grace is sufficient for you to handle this." "For my power is made perfect in weakness." In his weakness, Paul was forced to depend on God in the struggle with this demonic force that was coming against him. Paul says, "God's power was revealed to him in his weakness." That tells me that he received the power to overcome. "Therefore I will boast all the more gladly about my weaknesses, so that Christ's power may rest on me." Notice he doesn't say I will boast more gladly about my weaknesses so I can suffer more. We all need to depend on Him, like Paul, in our struggles against the demonic.

The thorn in Paul's flesh was a demonic attack, not a disease. A lot of people have used this "thorn in the flesh" concept to rationalize not getting healed. My pastor friend believed his brain tumor was a thorn in his flesh and was convinced it would kill him, and It did.

Chapter 16:

There's More Than One Way to Be Healed

When I talk to others about supernatural healing, I often encounter people with the question, "Is it wrong to go to the doctor? Is it a lack of faith?" My answer is of course not! I go to a great doctor. He is a believer and goes to our church. I thank God for doctors. But Christian doctors I've talked to, if they are honest, will say that while they can help in the healing process, it is God who is the healer! I mentioned earlier that I tore my rotator cuff and thank God for that surgeon. If I had been stupid and not gone to the doctor, I would be in a lot of pain right now. Some Christians look down upon other Christians who take medication, go to the doctor, or choose to have surgery, saying it is a lack of faith. Wrong!

As unconventional methods for healing have become increasingly popular, the question of pursuing these natural means of healing has also arisen: "Does alternative medicine displease God? Is using them a lack of faith?" Again, my answer is of course not! I go to a great chiropractor also a believer from our church. He has helped me dramatically. It is God who created all the herbs used in naturopathy, and it is He who gave them their healing properties. He pre-wired our bodies to heal themselves and He put everything we need to live healthy on this planet. Healing and divine health are His desire for us. He is a creative God and has made a creative people. There is definitely more than one way to be healed!

When I was pastoring a church in Grand Lake in the 1980s, several people were caught up in the extremes of the "Word of Faith" movement. Steve was one of my elders. He was a big burly biker, who had played football at Indiana University, and had several children. Their baby got really sick and was running a temperature between 104 and 105 degrees. They called me to their house to pray for the baby. I did pray but when the temperature did not come down I said: "Take that baby to the emergency room now."

They told me, "We are standing in faith, and we don't believe in doctors."

I knew their faith was genuine, but I shook my head and emphatically admonished them, "If you have a high temperature and are suffering, and you want to stand in faith for yourself, go ahead. But you better take that baby in now or I don't ever want to see you in our church again." Thankfully they did what I asked and the doctor successfully brought the baby's temperature into a normal range. The next day both Steve and his wife thanked me. Sometimes wisdom requires seeking medical attention as you continue to stand in faith for healing.

Does God heal through other believers?

I want to share two emails I got recently from our Healing Rooms. The first person wrote:

"I had a creative miracle. I went into the healing room for my swollen hand which looked like a balloon due to a wrist break. My hand was without much mobility. The kids and adults anointed me with oil and before their eyes, the swelling began to go down. The skin was changing in front of them. I received the ability to bring all my fingers to my thumb, which I couldn't do before. The swelling has continued to go down, the skin has continued changing. I am grateful to the kids and adults and that Jesus showed up in their prayers."

Isn't that exciting? I talked to one of the adults who had been present, and she said they all started screaming when they saw the hand shrinking. It is one thing to hear about a miracle happening but another thing to actually see it!

The second email came from a lady who went to the healing rooms on the same night. This lady had torn her ACL and wrote:

"I could not walk normally without a brace and now, after prayer, all the pain is gone and I can walk without the brace! The pain is 100% gone. I had both adults and children praying for me, they were awesome, Jesus is awesome!"

I share these testimonies to raise your faith level. These were not pastors but normal working people who love Jesus and love praying for people to be healed. The effectual fervent prayers of God's people (children as well as adults) avails much (James 5:16). I just want you to know that God is an incredible God. He loves us and He cares about us. Even if you have been going after healing and it hasn't happened yet, don't give up. Remember these testimonies and let your hope grow and let your faith in God's power to heal rise.

Matthew records the first words Jesus gives to His disciples. He commissions them before they were "born again" saying: "And as you go, preach, saying, 'The kingdom of heaven is at hand.' Heal the sick, cleanse the lepers, raise the dead, cast out demons. Freely you have received, freely give" (Matt. 10:7-8). Some of Jesus' last words are "...they will lay hands on the sick, and they will recover..." and they went out and preached everywhere, the Lord working with them and confirming the word through the accompanying signs. Amen" (Mark 16:18b, 20). If you step out in faith and pray for people and leave the results to Him, He will heal and bring people to Himself!

What if You Were a Follower of Jesus 2,000 Years Ago?

If you had been a follower of Jesus 2,000 years ago, you would have expected Him to reign politically, to break the power of Roman rule and taxation, and overthrow the government. Then suddenly when He was crucified, you would have become depressed and wanted to hide because you could be next. Jesus had told them that he wanted them to go out and proclaim the Good News, heal the sick and cast out demons. After His resurrection and before His ascension He told them, "I am going to accompany you with signs and wonders after I'm gone."

Now that Jesus had ascended to Heaven, He was asking His disciples to go out and convince a lost, dying, and skeptical world that He was alive. Remember most knew Jesus had been crucified. That was big news and a very public execution. Far fewer knew about His resurrection. This would be a daunting task wouldn't you say? You can't do that just through velvet voiced oratory.

Just recently my son, myself, and a former Vietnamese refugee, ministered to a group of teenage refugees. These young people, ages 14 – 20 years old had experienced a lot of trauma as they escaped from Burma (Myanmar). We started off by sharing words of knowledge and saw many physical and emotional healings occur. Then we shared our hearts on how God brings good out of even the worst trials.

His presence and love were so evident in the room that several gave their lives to Jesus. It wasn't the eloquence of our words that moved their hearts, but the living, breathing, power of God at work which convinced them He is alive!

Many times Leif Hetland and I have seen miraculous occurrences in Pakistan. We have seen blind eyes opened, limbs grow out, and a paralytic walk! The Koran says that Jesus was a miracle worker and a healer. Though they do not recognize Him as the Savior, even Muslims believe Jesus can heal. When we go to Pakistan, we don't call our meetings "Crusades" because that is not a good word for a Muslim. Christian Crusaders killed Muslims centuries ago and the word itself fosters prejudice and hatred. So instead we do "Healing Festivals" where Jesus shows up-He encounters people, and He heals them. Once He touches their hearts the walls come down and they have an open heart to receive Jesus. We've seen many Muslims become followers of Christ!

Just as He has with us, God will work with you and help you. He is an incredible God. Recently a man in our church told me he was flying back to Denver and a lady sat down next to him. God had given him a word of knowledge, and He felt he should pray for her healing. To her great joy, she was healed right there on the plane. She said she would never forget this moment. Turns out she was the pastor's wife of a large mega-church, and she said "Wow, God is Great!" You never know when you are going to have an opportunity to help people. People everywhere need God's touch.

Randy Clark taught me this: "When you pray for people, if you do it in love-if you really allow the love of Jesus to flow forth as well as the healing power-people will have a positive experience even if they don't get immediately healed." That is a great word and helps us have confidence to pray in faith, not worried about the outcome.

The result isn't up to us. We are not responsible for the healing, only for our obedience to pray!

Take Healing Beyond the Walls of the Church

I've been amazed at the percentage of unbelievers who get healed. I believe God cares so much about them; He bends over backward to heal them. In fact the most dramatic healings I've witnessed have been with unbelievers, especially Muslims. I have often found it is easier for unbelievers and people outside the church to be open to receive miraculous healing..

Don't let the fear of not seeing results block you from praying for those who don't believe. Evangelist Robby Dawkins has atheists pray for others to be healed, and when they see it happen, their theology changes instantly. God loves using these "foolish strategies" to get the job done (1 Cor. 1:27). Don't be afraid to step out. Faith is often spelled "RISK".

While writing this section, I received an email from Dan, the head of our Healing Rooms. Remarkably, we have been given permission to take healing teams to a local hospital. Dan wrote:

> "We prayed for a woman in the ER waiting room. She had an injured right shoulder and her whole arm was in pain and very swollen. She was new to Castle Rock and she asked what church we were from, and so we told her we were from The Rock (we don't tell unless they ask). Then, last Sunday, at the 11:00 am service during the greeting time, I turned around and there she was sitting two seats away. She had come to church to tell us that when she woke up the next

> morning, her arm was totally healed. No swelling, no pain, 100% normal. Praise God! She was quite emotional and thankful for her healing and I am excited that we send teams into the hospital. We get to work with all kinds of people both saved and unsaved."

God really is "Jehovah Rapha," the God who heals! Just before He was crucified, Jesus told us: "Very truly I tell you, whoever believes in me will do the works I have been doing, and they will do even greater things than these, because I am going to the Father" (John 14:12 NIV). He knew that all over the world, there would be Christians praying for the sick, more Christians than ever before. Do you know that in the last 25 years, more people have come into the Kingdom than in all of history since Jesus resurrected from the dead. Do you know the body of Christ spreads all over the world and the healing power of Jesus is being released especially in places like China, India, Thailand, Pakistan, Africa, South America, etc. God is doing amazing things and we should be so grateful to be alive at this time. It is even happening in the United States with greater frequency now as well!

To be honest with you, the greatest healing is when a person receives Jesus Christ as Lord and Savior, because that not only has temporal value but it is an eternal reality! If you died tonight and are not sure you would be in Heaven, you can have an assurance. Jesus died for your sins, and He wants you to receive that sacrifice and invite Him into your life. Sin, condemnation and guilt are all removed when you pray from the heart: "Jesus, thank You for giving Your life for me. Now please forgive my sins and come into my life." Put it in your own words, He hears your heart.

Maybe you are saying, "Well pastor, I did give my life to Him before, but I have strayed away." I want you to know His arms of love are just waiting for you to come back. Speak to Him now. Invite Him back into your life. He loves you so much! He has been waiting patiently for this moment. "And this is the testimony: "God has given us eternal life, and this life is in his Son (Jesus). Whoever has the Son has life; whoever does not have the Son of God does not have life. I write these things to you who believe in the name of the Son of God so that you may know that you have eternal life" (1 John 5:11-13 NIV). Now that you have the assurance of your salvation settled, I want to pray this prayer over you:

"Heavenly Father, I pray for each and every person reading this. Please give them courage to not only receive healing, but also to release healing to others. Anoint them for the task ahead and give them the courage to recognize and act on opportunities to pray for healing and to lead people to Christ. Holy Spirit we leave the results to you. Amen!"

Section 7

HEALING OF THE EMOTIONS

"To ignore, repress, or dismiss our feelings is to fail to listen to the stirrings of the Spirit. Within our emotional life... Unhealed emotions can stifle growth, but freedom comes when the Holy Spirit delivers us from the lies that attempt to bind us with emotional chains."

- Brennan Manning

Past wounds and hurts often try to haunt us for a lifetime. They pull us down emotionally, robbing our peace and joy and limiting our ability to love. Thank God for the Holy Spirit's power to set us free.

Chapter 17:

Emotional and Physical Healing

Jesus came to heal the brokenhearted (Luke 4:18). God wants us to be whole. He cares about every aspect of our lives. God has pleasure in the prosperity of His servant" (Psalm 35:27). Some teachers use this scripture to tell people God wants to make them wealthy–especially if they will give money into their ministry! But the Hebrew word, prosperity, translated here is "*shalom*." It means "wholeness, peace, and well being in every area of your life." Isn't that beautiful? God cares about our wholeness spiritually, physically, emotionally, relationally, financially, and in every possible way. The NIV translation is even more clear. It says God "delights in the well being of His servant."

3 John 2 says, "I pray you will prosper in all things and be in health just as your soul prospers." The Greek word, prosper, in the original translation is "*euodoo*." That comes from two Greek words "*eu*" = meaning "well" and "*hodos*" meaning "way or journey". Thus John was praying that everything in life's journey would go well, and be accompanied by wholeness.

Another place in scripture where it shows how God cares about our whole being puts it this way: "May God himself, the God who makes everything holy and whole, put you together – spirit, soul, and body – and keep you fit for the coming of our Master, Jesus Christ" (1 Thess. 5:23-24 MSG). This translation says, "make you holy and whole." The problem is when we see the word "holy," we often think it means perfection. We think Holy means being a little more spiritual than everybody else. The word "holy" is the Greek word "*hagios*" or "*hagiosmos*" depending on whether it is an adjective or a noun. It means to be set apart, totally sold out, focused (on Him).

Holy is not a condition of being perfect or not making a mistake. Holy is being focused on Him so He becomes the center of our life. That is when He can begin to make us whole, because of His love for us working in us. God wants us complete in every area of our lives. He cares about us that much. It goes on to say, "The One who called you is completely dependable. If He said it, He'll do it" (v. 28). Rest assured, He will keep His Word and fulfill every promise. This may not mean He does it overnight, or as fast as you think He ought to, but He will do it over time. Jesus demonstrated that grace when He hung on the cross, showing His great love for us. We can't earn His grace; it comes to us freely, so we can only receive it. Let's be grateful!

Kris Valloton's Story

Kris Valloton is one of the pastors from Bethel Church in Redding, California. Recently, he spoke at our church. He told a story about how he had a really difficult childhood. His father had attempted to drown him when he was three years old, and his mother struggled emotionally. His parents divorced, but his mother re-married a violent, abusive man, and Kris's life became even rougher. She divorced this second husband when Kris was 15, and things got even worse.

They were living in the San Francisco Bay area and a prowler kept trying to break into their house. Things got so bad they actually screwed their windows shut for safety, however, in the summer with no open windows and no air conditioning, it would be sweltering and suffocating. This prowler had tried to get in several times, and fear of his entry had made their lives miserable. Kris said it was so hot, one day he finally unscrewed his window.

It was peaceful for a couple of days, but the next night the guy came into the house through his window. The stalker went into his mother's bedroom and traumatized her and Kris. From then on, his mom slept with a shotgun, and he slept with a .22 caliber rifle. Kris' Mom was very distraught, and she had psoriasis all over her body. She itched continually and looked terrible. Her life was so miserable that he would hear her crying herself to sleep each night.

At 15 years old Kris said he really didn't believe in God, but he was so desperate for his mother that he cried out and said, "God, if you are there, if you are God or whoever You are, if You will heal my mother, emotionally and physically, I will serve You the rest of my life."

Kris shares that he heard an audible voice that said, "I am Jesus Christ and it is done."

The next morning his mother came out smiling. She was so happy and at peace. Miraculously, the psoriasis had left her body. Kris said he was more surprised than anyone. A week later, Jesus spoke to him and said, "I have done what you asked; now I am waiting for you to serve me." Soon after that Kris gave his life to Jesus. Prior to this, Kris' mother had been a nominal believer, but after she was healed became on-fire for the Lord! Their lives were dramatically transformed through that miracle healing. If God will do this for Kris' mother, He will do it for you!

God doesn't show favoritism. He doesn't limit who He heals to rich or poor, saved or unsaved, Jew or Greek–He wants to do this for all. Healing is demonstrated throughout the entire Bible and I have shared many passages with you. In this section we will focus on emotional healing. Sometimes people will press into God for physical healing and just accept emotional turmoil and dysfunction as something they will have to live with. Not true! God wants to heal your damaged emotions. Sometimes it happens as quickly and powerfully as it did with Kris' mom. Often, I have found it can take years for God to completely free someone emotionally. I've experienced a lot of emotional healing, but He is still working on me!

The Most Difficult Area to Heal

If you live on planet Earth, you will have damaged emotions; you can't help it. I had struggled emotionally as a child, and I am still dealing with some of these problems. I had a difficult birth, almost dying, and was pulled from my mother's womb with forceps, which crushed my head. My dad told me many times that I was the ugliest baby in the nursery. My mom was heavily sedated, and my dad was in the military, so I felt abandoned from birth. I was sexually abused by a babysitter several times. when I was about four. I was sickly and often missed school. My dad was an orphan and had his own emotional issues. He was traveling all the time, so we had no relationship at all. My mom was gone all day so I felt forsaken and unimportant.

God heals damaged emotions, but seldom does this happen instantaneously or automatically. I pulled out an old book by David Seamands called, *Healing for Damaged Emotions*. He writes:

> "We preachers have often given people the mistaken idea that new birth and being filled with the Spirit are going to automatically take care of these emotional struggles and hang-ups. But that just isn't true. A great salvation experience of Jesus Christ is important and is eternally valuable but this is not a short cut to emotional health. It is not a quick cure for personality struggles. Understanding that salvation does not give instant emotional health offers us important insight into the doctrine of sanctification. It is impossible to know how a Christian person truly feels merely on the basis of their outward behavior."

When you are "born again," at the point you received Jesus Christ, you instantaneously come alive to God in your human spirit to God. The Holy Spirit comes to live in you; you begin a relationship with the Father and with Jesus. Sanctification is the <u>process</u> where, over time we are becoming more like Jesus. Sometimes it is a painful process, and David Seamands clearly points this out so well.

When I first got saved, my life was a disaster. I was strung out on drugs, had several broken sexual relationships with women, and no sense of purpose in my life. I was also dabbling in the occult and was channeling "ancient spirits" (which turned out to be demons!) At the time I was heading up the Monterey Zendo (a place where people would meditate).To be honest when Jesus came into my life, things were in a downward spiral.

I remember hearing a message a few months later that if you are saved and filled with the Spirit, then you should not have any more serious problems or struggles. This made me feel really condemned, and I wondered, what is wrong with me? But that was a lie. Nothing was wrong with me. I was perfectly normal. I was saved, and my spirit was new, but my flesh still needed the process of sanctification. We must have compassion for each other and for ourselves when we are going through various kinds of emotional struggles.

Dr. Seamands also writes: "It is necessary that we understand this [sanctification process]. First of all, so that we can compassionately live with ourselves and allow the Holy Spirit to work with special healing in our own hurts and confusion. We also need to understand this in order to not judge other people too harshly, but to have patience with their confusing and contradictory behavior. In so doing, we will be kept from unfairly criticizing and judging fellow Christians." It is sad when Christians judge and put down other Christians who are having emotional problems. When people struggle, they don't need to be condemned on top of it. Understand that God is a compassionate, healing God. He is a God that heals us: spirit, soul and body. He cares about every part of us. When we ignore or remain in denial of our damaged emotions, we produce anxiety, depression and addiction.

Mary Magdalene appears 18 times in the New Testament. Although the Bible never states that Mary was a prostitute, history portrays her this way. The Jewish Talmud mentions the town of Magdalene was known for its sexual promiscuity. Also, Mary was probably single since she is identified by the town she is from, not her husband's name. Sexual promiscuity (along with abuse and many other things) often opens the door to the demonic. Jesus cast 7 demons out of Mary (Lk. 8:2) and she becomes one of his most faithful followers. She is there when Pontius Pilot condemns Jesus. She is near the cross supporting Jesus at his crucifixion and she is the first one to the empty tomb! Obviously she received emotional healing and deliverance which redeemed her life in a transforming way!

Early in my first pastorate in Grand Lake, we were ministering to a young girl who began manifesting demons. She even fell on the floor and slithered like a snake. A lady from the island of Trinidad understood the demonic well. She helped this girl receive forgiveness from her sexual sins. She was totally set free and no longer tormented by demons.

It is much harder to talk with someone about emotional pain than physical pain. Feelings of guilt or shame can make it hard to admit that something is wrong. If you had a broken arm, you would go get an x-ray. When you find yourself with irrational responses, unexplained hostility, feelings of hopelessness, or anxiety, diagnosis is not as simple as that x-ray nor is treatment as clear as setting a bone and putting it in a cast.

There is much scientific evidence that emotional pain and its effect on our thoughts weakens our immune system and leads to physical illness and disease.[1] Toxic emotions literally change the shape of DNA strands and allow disease and infirmity free access to your body's cells.[2] The mind, emotions, and body are all closely and intricately linked. It is vital for you to understand this in order for you to be whole in your soul (3 John 2). Your soul is made up of your mind, your will, <u>and your emotions</u>. God wants your emotions to be healed!

Remember the story of the paralytic who was lowered through the roof (Mark 2)? Well Jesus first told the man his sins were forgiven. We can only imagine what freedom this brought to someone who probably had emotional issues and maybe even shame. Then Jesus heals him physically and points out to the Pharisees that the first step was harder than the second.

Facing the root cause of your emotional trauma is a huge first step. Carrying guilt, shame or disappointment can hinder you from receiving healing in these areas. You must come to the place where you know beyond a shadow of doubt that God loves you unconditionally and forgives and accepts you completely. Sometimes without meaning to, we can shift the blame for our emotional state to God. This blaming God is in itself a huge block to emotional healing. It puts up a thick wall of emotional defenses that can block us from receiving His love and healing power.

Jesus carried your sorrows on the cross – He bore your grief, pain, and affliction (Isa. 53:4). You have no need to continue to carry what He has already willingly carried for you. Let Him have it. Let Him bear your burden and heal your grief. "Cast all your cares upon Him, for He cares for you" (1 Pet. 5:7). Whether it comes all at once in a miraculous display of God's power, or slowly and steadily through a gentle progression of His tender nurture and care, God's desire for you is to have total and complete healing in your emotions. Be free!

---

[1] See work by Dr. Herbert Benson, MD, president of Harvard Medical School's Mind-Body Institute, http://www.massgeneral.org/bhi/research/). [2] *Who Switched Off My Brain* by Dr. Caroline Leaf. © 2009 by Thomas Nelson.

Chapter 18:

Destiny's Enemy

Barriers to our Destiny

Insecurity, low self-esteem, childhood wounds, perfectionism, shame and fear can keep people from fulfilling their destiny. These are all barriers that hinder us from moving forward in our lives. These feelings have tried to rob me from my destiny as well. Lies become embedded in our emotions. For example, my dad was a traveling salesman and was gone all week, and my mom owned a shop, leaving me with nannies or baby sitters. When she came home at night she would drink a lot and check out. Because they were absent, I felt abandoned and unloved.

But Jesus revealed to me in a Theophostic[1] counseling session that as their first child my parents loved me deeply, but were preoccupied with trying to make a living. They were impacted by the Depression and World War II and poured themselves into providing financially but not emotionally. I realized that they worried about me and loved me deeply. I saw how Jesus was very close to me when they were not around. The destructive thought pattern of feeling unloved was given new light, a new perspective – literally rerouted by the Holy Spirit.

Theophostic counseling and/ or SOZO[2] sessions have helped me so much bringing inner healing. Meeting with a counselor who knows how to operate by the Holy Spirit can also help us so to become more emotionally healthy. The anxiety and depression caused by my past is slowly fading away! Satan is the "father of lies" (John 8:44) and uses these lies to put barriers between us and our loving Father God.

I love Luke. A disciple of Jesus, Luke was also a physician, and really understood the need for both emotional and physical healing. He wrote both the Gospel of Luke and the Book of Acts. He told many stories which illustrate the power of Jesus to heal One story is about a guy named Zacchaeus. (We would sing to our kids a song about Zacchaeus and how he was a "wee little man"). Zacchaeus was in fact a little guy – not tall enough to see Jesus in the crowd. Zacchaeus really wanted to encounter Jesus when He came to town, so he climbed a tree. When Jesus saw him up in the tree, He called him by name. He said, "Zacchaeus, come down out of that tree. Tonight I am coming to your house for dinner."

As soon as Jesus spoke those words, religious people got upset because Zacchaeus was a crook. They asked each other: "How Jesus could be going to a sinner's house?" They hated Zacchaeus because he was the chief tax collector. Tax collectors were despised because they extracted hard earned money from the people and lived a life of luxury. Zacchaeus was wealthy, and probably flaunted his wealth. We don't know if he had a Napoleon, "little man", complex, but he probably loved the power, position, and wealth which made him feel better despite his size and insecurity. People grumbled about Jesus going to his house, but Jesus came for the lost, not the ones who thought they had it all together.

When He got to his house, Zacchaeus had an encounter with Jesus which transformed him and so he said, "I will give half of my money to the poor and for anyone I have cheated in any way, I will pay them back four times what I cheated them." When Jesus saw such a change of heart, He excitedly proclaimed: "Today salvation has come to this house because this man too is a son of Abraham for the Son of Man came to seek and to save the lost." (Luke 19:9-10) When Jesus says "salvation," it is the Greek word "*sozo*" which includes emotional healing. Zaccheus' life was changed by that meeting with the Lord Jesus Christ. Encounters with Jesus change us forever!

The encounter Saul of Tarsus had with Jesus on the road to Damascus totally changed his life. When we encounter the one who is love and grace, it changes our life too. We start to see the old garbage in our life in a new light as it begins to fall away. It is a process by which the Holy Spirit begins to heal us and change us from the inside out. Lies are brought to the light and destroyed by love and truth. Pause right now and invite Jesus to touch any area of your life that is emotionally out of whack. He will come! Even better if you sense damaged emotions look for SOZO or "Theophostic" therapy in your area. (See the endnotes from this chapter for more information.)

I have seen significant emotional healing in people's lives over the years. Several years ago we took a young girl into our lives who had been satanically heavily abused. We walked with her through some very traumatic times, and saw her make great strides toward wholeness. Deep trauma like that takes time to heal. In life we go through a lot of struggles. Jesus comes by the Holy Spirit and helps us when we are open and desperate.

My Battle with Anxiety

Over the past 2-1/2 years I have had an intense battle with anxiety. I had minor bouts with anxiety in the past, but nothing like what I've experienced during these last few years. Let me share an excerpt from my journal written about a year and a half ago.

> "I can't get above this anxiety; it seems to tie me in knots robbing my peace, my joy, my hope and my ability to love. I keep seeing negative future consequences. Why? Is it because I'm getting older, losing my passion, or am I losing my mind? Sometimes it seems dark and depressing, like I am in a dark pit and can't climb out. But usually it is fear that seems to grip me during the day and in the middle of the night, robbing my sleep. I pray, quote scriptures, rebuke the devil, pray in the Spirit, exercise fervently – but nothing seems to permanently break this horrible anxiety. Oh sometimes temporary relief comes, but soon it's back like an unwanted enemy. Help me, Lord – I'm sinking and hurting!"

As I read this passage from my journal, it brought back a lot of those feelings. I wanted to leave the ministry and just go live on a beach somewhere. But the Lord and my wife convinced me the anxiety would just follow me there. For the last 2-1/2 years I have been counseling with a "theophostic" counselor who has helped tremendously. Jesus has revealed many lies from my childhood and healed past traumas. The anxiety started when my long time friend and our executive pastor retired. Fortunately, my son left a lucrative development job in Houston to become the new executive pastor by my side. This helped more than he could ever know. He is doing a great job!

Also, my daughter Anna, who has tremendous insight through the Holy Spirit, has helped me so much. We've had many phone calls and visits where she has uncovered lies from my past. I am so grateful to both our children!

Am I totally free from anxiety? No, but I am about 80% freer than I was. Life is so much better. The peace, joy, hope and love have returned back to my life. Jesus is closer, and I seem to have more empathy for people, especially those struggling in any way. Jesus is the one who transforms us and gives us more compassion for those who are going through similar struggles. He turns our struggles to good even though it is not fun when we are going through those trials. The Apostle Paul said it well that the Holy Spirit: "comforts us in all our tribulation that we may be able to comfort those who are in any trouble, with the comfort with which we ourselves are comforted by God." (2 Cor 1:4)

My youngest brother, Guy, was a tremendous support to me during this time. He had observed and struggled with anxiety while working with the homeless in New York City. My middle brother, Peter, who has always been the picture of calm success, helped to anchor me with his practical suggestions. Not to mention the one who helped the most, my wonderful wife, Yvonne, who endured the pain I put her through, and loved and supported me this entire time. I am so blessed with an incredible family. Thanks – I wouldn't have made it without all of you.

Deliverance = Freedom from Every Oppression

Jesus goes on to preach that He came "To proclaim liberty to the captives...and to set at liberty those who are oppressed" (Luke 4:18). There are so many things in this world that try to captivate and oppress us such as: addiction to drugs, alcohol, sex, money, and power just to name a few. Workaholics fall into this category too. If someone hurts us we can become captive to bitterness. Jesus is the one who sets us free! Sometimes He does it in our own trials, sometimes through other people, and sometimes directly freeing us.

What is oppression? It isn't people. We don't wrestle against people. Oppression comes from the enemy. His name is Satan, and he has a hierarchy of oppressive agents . "We are not fighting against flesh-and-blood enemies, but against evil rulers and authorities of the unseen world, against mighty powers in this dark world, and against evil spirits in the heavenly places" (Eph 6:12 NLT).

Although sometimes demons can motivate people to come against us, our battle is against the elements of Satan's hierarchy. He heads up this network of fallen angels and demons. This is where oppression originates.

Evil rulers and Authorities (Principalities)

Evil rulers and principalities (authorities) are fallen angels who have become the territorial demonic princes over assigned areas. For example, an angel of the Lord came to Daniel to explain why the answer to his prayer was delayed for 21 days. It was because of a fallen angelic prince who was over the territory of Persia that interfered with Daniel's prayers. The angel said to Daniel, "Do not fear, Daniel, for from the first day that you set your heart to understand,

and to humble yourself before your God, your words were heard; and I have come because of your words. But the prince of the kingdom of Persia withstood me twenty-one days; and behold, Michael, one of the chief princes, came to help me, for I had been left alone there with the kings of Persia. (Daniel 10:12-13) Interestingly, the demonic "Prince of Persia" is still active today. Look at all the problems in the Iran/Iraq area of the world which is present day Persia.

Mighty Powers (in this dark world)

The next part of this hierarchy was mighty powers. These demonic forces have less power than those mentioned prior. However, they are strongmen who are in command over other lesser demons to do damage. Jesus refers to binding "the strong man" in order to take control. A "mighty power" could be a strong man or ruling demon (Mark 3:27).

Evil Spirits or Demons

Last are evil spirits or demons that inhabit our atmosphere. Most of us don't come in contact with Satan or territorial princes but lesser demons are the ones who harass us. As Christians they attack our minds and emotions since they do not have access to our redeemed human spirit. Often the thoughts and feelings we are having come from those demons that subtly get us to accept their thoughts as our own. They play on our emotional weaknesses. This is where oppression comes from.

You Win!

Demons can never possess (take over a person's whole being) believers in Jesus Christ, they can only oppress them. Oppression simply means demonic pressure (or attack) on the mind, emotions, and physical body, but not the human spirit which is born again. We need to be aware of the enemy's tactics. The Apostle Peter understood this when he wrote: "Stay alert! Watch out for your great enemy, the devil. He prowls around like a roaring lion, looking for someone to devour. Stand firm against him, and be strong in your faith." (I Pet. 5:8-9a). Notice he is like a roaring lion, using fear, intimidation and lies – this is all he has available to harass you with since Jesus defeated him.

Ultimately, Jesus has already won the victory for you. It is a completed, finished work. Even though it is already accomplished in the heavenlies, you must walk out the reality here on earth. Remember that the enemy who battles against you is already condemned for eternity (John 16:11) He has no legal rights over you as a child of God. He cannot pluck you from the Father's hand (Isa. 43:13). Though the enemy makes a lot of noise and seems formidable, his authority is restricted (Heb. 2:14). Jesus is your constant advocate (1 John 2:1) and the Holy Spirit constantly makes intercession for you (Rom. 8:26). Satan's power is limited and God's power is limitless! But you must appropriate this victory; through Christ you win!

---

[1] Theophostic counseling comes from "*Theo*" (God) and "*phostic*" (light). It was developed in 1996 by Ed Smith and is an approach to mind renewal and the healing of emotional pain. Theophostic Prayer Ministries is one of the fastest growing inner healing ministries in evangelical churches the United States. Source: The Christian Research Institute, *Theophostic Prayer Ministry (Part One)* Article ID JAT206-1 by Elliot Miller. Retrieved from http://www.equip.org/article/theophostic-prayer-ministry-part-one/ on 9/13/2-16.

[2] SOZO is a unique inner healing and deliverance ministry birthed at Bethel Church in Redding, California. It comes from the Greek word "sozo" (saved, healed, delivered). It is not counseling, but a time of interacting with the Father, Son and Holy Spirit for wholeness and freedom. SOZO is aimed to get to the root of what's hindering your personal connection with God. Source: SOZO Retrieved from: http://www.bethelsozo.com on 9/13/16

Chapter 19:

The Keys to Being Set Free!

Understanding Our Authority

When you received Jesus, you immediately had an adversary (Satan means adversary), and he and his demons were pitted against you. Don't whine about it because *"greater is He that is in you than he who is in the world."* (1 John 4:4) Jesus has given us authority over the enemy, so when he and his demons attack, we get stronger and learn how to battle. Sometimes temporary oppression can come upon a believer where the enemy will take some of the emotional wounds and use these as avenues to attack. The Holy Spirit will often bring light revealing from where the oppression is coming. Realize the enemy will not be able to keep you bound, because Jesus is greater and has already defeated him at Calvary. However, you can't remain passive. You must go on the offensive.

There are several times in the New Testament where Jesus or the disciples broke demon possession or oppression. There is an instance where the disciples were unable to cast out a demon so Jesus had to. He told them that this type of demon only came out by "prayer and fasting." In other words they needed to get serious about it and not be distracted. Prayer and fasting increases our focus and can increase our anointing and authority because we become more closely connected to God, Jesus, and the Holy Spirit!

Interestingly, Jesus' first instructions to the disciples included casting out demons (Matthew 10:8). Also, just before Jesus ascended into Heaven to sit at the right hand of the Father, He gave the disciples instructions. He said: "And these signs will follow those who believe (all believers); in my name they will cast out demons ..." (Mark 16:17a)

When I went to pastor in Grand Lake, Colorado after graduating from seminary, I ran into several demonic situations. Seminary had not prepared me for these at all. In the halls of higher learning there is a lot of ignorance about the demonic. Often Christians ignore the demonic, thinking Jesus' victory on the cross automatically preserves them from a demonic attack. Fortunately, Ephesians 6 sets the record straight. A demon can oppress a believer; that is when we need to take authority over that oppressive spirit. Never cast a demon out of a person who has not received Christ or the end result will be worse. If you do take authority over the demonic, make sure you lead them to Jesus to fill the empty place.

When you see the word "save" or "saved", "heal" or "deliver" it is all from the Greek New Testament word: "*sozo*". This word means to save spiritually, and to heal emotionally and physically. It also means to deliver from danger or from the demonic. This small Greek word also means "to make whole" because God wants us to walk in wholeness, spirit, soul, and body free from demonic oppression.

A few years ago I was ministering at a YWAM Discipleship Training School in Denver. I was starting to pray for a young man from Australia when I sensed in the Spirit that there was a demon that looked like a deformed, ugly monkey on his shoulders. I didn't see it with my eyes but discerned it with my spirit. I felt this strong anointing of power come on me. I took my arms and wrapped them very loosely around his head and shoulders. Then I commanded the demon to go and flung my arms out as the Holy Spirit directed breaking the demonic power. The fellow went flying through the air about six feet backwards and fell into some chairs. I thought *Oh no, now I've really done it. I have injured the poor guy!*

He lay there for about 15 seconds, but then got up with a huge smile raising his hand in the air and said "I am free!" I was so relieved. He told everyone that he had been involved in the occult before he became a believer and seemed to labor under a weight of destructive feelings and thoughts. I led him in a short prayer of repentance, and he received total forgiveness from Jesus. Two days later I talked with him again, and he said he felt so close to God and so totally free. We thanked the Lord together!

At the Rock, we have a lot of ways that people can work toward wholeness. We have a whole list, starting with "Sozo" therapy, "Theophostic" ministry, and several Spirit- led counselors. In all these instances, Jesus is the primary source of healing by the power of the Holy Spirit which breaks the lies and wounds setting people free. This usually involves a process towards freedom. We also have Celebrate Recovery[1] which is focused primarily on addictions of any kind. We have Healing Rooms[2] the first and third Tuesday of the month for both physical and emotional healing as well as altar ministry where people can receive prayer after every service.

Recently in a service I explained demonic oppression and had anyone stand who was sensing it. I was amazed that over half the people stood in both services. I prayed the prayer below, and many told me they experienced new freedom. If you feel any oppression, pray this prayer as though I am praying with you. Be blessed.

> *"Father, right now in the name of Jesus, I take authority over every oppressive spirit that would try to come and rob my God given destiny. Enemy, you have no authority. I say in the name of Jesus, that you have to go. I break every lie and oppression now in Jesus Name, and I thank You for Your blood which covers me. Thank You Father, in the name of Jesus, that you now download peace, strength, truth and Your love, which I freely receive, along with a new freedom!"*

Now just breathe in that freedom. Pause quietly. It is yours. Praise Him for your freedom! Thank Him for victory!

It is important to realize that once we recognize oppression, we can see it is not coming from inside us. We realize it is beyond our natural feelings or circumstances, but not beyond Jesus. So operating in the authority of Jesus Christ is the power that breaks oppression over us. Awareness is the first step. Then we can follow through. Remember, you have the same authority that I have over the demonic. Don't hesitate to pray with another believer to be set free. Remember, "one can put 1,000 to flight and two can put 10,000 to flight (Deut. 32:30) "And Jesus said to them, 'I saw Satan fall like lightning from heaven.[19] Behold, I give you the authority to trample on serpents and scorpions, and over all the power of the enemy, and nothing shall by any means hurt you'" (Luke 10:18-19).

Dealing With a Suicidal Spirit

A spirit of suicide comes from Satan and the demonic because he desires "to steal, kill and destroy you." (John 10:10). I have been able to not only break spirits of suicide over people, but help people to recognize it is not their mind, but the source is a demon conjuring up this destructive act. It is that demonic spirit trying to convince them to do harm to themselves. That is why Peter said, "Stay alert! Watch out for your great enemy, the devil" (1 Pet. 5:8). When we realize these are enemy thoughts, we can stand against them and be victorious. "Resist him firm in your faith!" (1 Peter 5:9) We need to be active in our resistance not passive. "Submit yourselves, then, to God. Resist the devil, and he will flee from you" (James 4:7 NIV).

A couple of years ago I was preaching on this, and a few Sundays later a boy about 17 years old came to me and asked to talk privately. He told me for two years he had thoughts of taking his own life. In fact, he said twice he had come close to following through. Then he said "Since you had talked about where those thoughts come from, I have been able to resist them immediately, and they leave me." I hooked him up with one of our Spirit-filled counselors who dealt with some emotional issues from his childhood, and he is doing so well! He learned where the thoughts originated, and how he could take those thoughts captive. "The weapons we fight with are not the weapons of the world. On the contrary, they have divine power to demolish strongholds. We demolish arguments and every pretension that sets itself up against the knowledge of God, and we <u>take captive</u> every thought to make it obedient to Christ" (2 Cor. 10:4-5 NIV).

One of the keys to becoming emotionally whole is forgiveness. I mentioned before that I was sexually abused by a baby sitter when I was 4 years old. It took a few sessions, but I was able to forgive this emotionally sick woman, who had probably been abused in her childhood. I also had to forgive my mother for dropping me off at her home several times, ignoring my screams and pleas not to leave me there. Forgiveness frees us – thank you Jesus for empowering us to forgive!

The Power of Forgiveness

Forgiveness helps to release healing both emotionally and physically and is often the key to bringing wholeness. You have to forgive, it is not an option. Kris Valloton (from Bethel Church) explained that he went through another very hard time a few years ago. Bill Johnson, the head pastor, got sick and had to scale back, so Kris took on some of his commitments which caused him to become overwhelmed.

Then Kris' son came to him in tears and said that his wife had left, and they were going through a horrendous divorce. It brought back all the feelings of what his mother had gone through, and he said that he ended up on his couch for six months and couldn't get off it. He felt paralyzed by depression. But, during that time, he began to heal when he realized he had to forgive his step-father. Then he had to forgive the spouse of his son. He had to release it from his heart, and when he did, God began to heal him. Today I think he is one of the most powerful speakers in the country, because he is not afraid to share his struggles and what came out of them.

In David Seamand's book, *Healing for Damaged Emotions*, he talks about a boy who had a father who insisted he get all A's in school. He would get A's and B's and an occasional C. He worked really hard and finally got all A's. He ran proudly to his Dad to show him his report card, but his Dad said, "I know all those teachers, and they give out A's like candy." In effect, he belittled his son's achievement and told him that he hadn't really accomplished much at all. The boy grew up to be a pastor, but felt he could never please his congregation. He always felt he was falling short. Then he had a nervous breakdown and had to leave the ministry. He went through a very difficult time of depression. He felt oppressed and was an emotional wreck.

Gradually, through Spirit-led counseling, he began to climb out of the pit of despair. He forgave his father and received great emotional healing and freedom from oppression, but it took over a year. The "rest of the story" is that he went back into ministry with a whole new outlook and has helped many people who were emotionally distraught. He especially was able to help those who always felt they could not live up to whatever standard was expected. God sets us free so we can free others!

My Youngest Brother Set Free

Perhaps one of the most dramatic stories of the power of forgiveness was conveyed to me by my youngest brother whose name is Guy. Guy had a difficult childhood and struggled with alcohol, anxiety and depression. He wound up in New York City, working at a rescue mission helping the homeless. The Holy Spirit came into his room at a low point and gave him a vision about how to help them.

God showed Guy how to really impact the homeless in New York City. He started a foundation called "We Can," where he was able to set up "reclamation centers" around New York City hiring all homeless people. A New York bottle bill gave 5 cents for any empty bottle or can. But there was a problem. Homeless people couldn't redeem their cans and bottles in Manhattan since many of the store-keepers didn't allow these dirty, smelly people in their establishments and had no room for storage.

Guy set up reclamation centers where they could bring the cans and bottles and receive money. This gave homeless people a sense of independence, a source of income, and a feeling of self worth. It also helped to clean up New York City. As a result he spoke on *Good Morning America* several times and many other television programs.

He spoke twice to the Harvard business school and was honored in many ways, receiving many awards. He did this for 25 years and literally changed the course of history in New York City. But, there is something that came very close to derailing him and destroying his life in the midst of his success.

Our mother died when she was only 69 years old, and my dad remarried. The person he remarried was not a nice person. In fact, she was an evil person, bent on taking my father's money and keeping his three sons from seeing him. For some reason, she especially hated my brother Guy with an intense hatred. She kept him from the house, even though he lived only an hour away, and would not let my Father see him or talk with him. This was before cell phones, so calling the home phone number was the only option. She wouldn't take any phone calls from us and destroyed all the family photos. Basically, she cut him off from his sons (and particularly Guy) in every way, shape and form.

My brother Guy got so upset and angry about this that he thought up ways to kill her. One of the ways he thought of was: "If I just taser her, she will have a heart attack, and it will look like she died of a heart attack." Now, I know that sounds sickly humorous in a way, but he thought of all these ways because he was consumed with this hatred for her. He thought about revenge morning, noon, and night. It started to take a toll on "We Can," the foundation he was running to help the homeless. The constant thoughts created by this hatred overwhelmed him. He couldn't sleep at night. He wasn't able to eat well, and it began affecting his physical, mental and emotional health.

Finally in his struggle, he went to a Catholic Priest, who also worked with the homeless, and did confession. Now, Guy is a believer but not Catholic. Yet he told me what a great guy this priest was and how his insight changed Guy's life and saved We Can.

The priest told him: "What I want you to do is to picture your stepmother, who you hate so much, during her early childhood." He continued, "You know that hatred will totally destroy your life if you don't deal with it. And, here is how I want you to handle it. I want you to, over the next seven days, take each day and visualize this lady. Start first with when she was a newborn baby, and then the next day focus on when she was six months old. And then the next day maybe when she was three years old, then when she was six years old and then right up to when she was a teenager. Each day that you do that, I want you to pour liquid love over her like honey. It may take several hours each day to be able to do this, but don't give up."

Guy told me that it was really hard, but he did it. He said that the first night took him four hours and several times he cried out saying: "God, please help me."He visually poured God's love over her. And, then he did it again the next day. He saw some things, like how she was abused in her childhood. He said that at the end of seven days, not only did he not hate her, but he said that he felt this incredible compassion and love for her. He felt sorry for her. This process not only surprised him, but totally broke the hatred, bitterness and anger that he had in his heart toward her. It literally transformed his life! Another amazing thing happened as a result of this heart change. Instead of going under, We Can began to thrive, having an even greater impact on the city.

Something else transpired that was equally amazing and prophetic. The Catholic priest told Guy: "On the seventh day, I want you to call your father at 5:00 pm.

My brother answered, "I won't get through. "She won't let me through."

The priest reiterated: "Just call at 5:00 pm."

Well on that seventh day Guy called at 5:00 pm, and supernaturally he got through and our dad answered the phone. He explained that his wife was in the hospital and was not there, so miraculously, Guy got to talk to our dad. He immediately left New York and drove down and saw our dad for the first time in several years. They had a great time together. He called me in Colorado, and I flew in the next day. Our middle brother, Peter, came in from Massachusetts. We had such a fun time together.

Dad asked us if we would help him get free from this woman. He told us how difficult it had been being trapped. So I took him with me back to Colorado. We helped with divorce proceedings. Ironically, when dad was dying, Guy became his caretaker and they became very close. They had not gotten along growing up, but they came to love each other. None of this would ever have happened if my brother, Guy, had not forgiven from his heart. He looks back at that time as a turning point of his life. He said he also realized it was Jesus through the Holy Spirit that empowered him to be able to forgive. He said "I could never forgive her in my own power. I was consumed with hatred, and I felt justified in hating her."

Let me encourage you, if you have any hatred or bitterness in your heart, (even a small amount), please deal with it. It won't affect that other person, but it will mess you up a lot. *Get rid of all bitterness, rage, anger, harsh words, and slander, as well as all types of evil behavior. Instead, be kind to each other, tenderhearted, <u>forgiving</u> one another, just as God through Christ has forgiven you.* (Eph 4:31-32 NLT)

To get rid of all bitterness, rage, anger, etc… and "become tender hearted, and forgive one another is close to impossible in our own strength. We need help! That is why Paul goes on to say that the way we forgive is just as God forgave through Christ who has forgiven us. If we focus on the magnitude of sin we have been forgiven of, it helps to empower us to forgive others. Jesus helps us dramatically by the power of the Holy Spirit. That doesn't mean it is easy or instantaneous.

Forgiving someone else is often like peeling a Bermuda onion. You take that first step to forgive and you think, "I'm now free of bitterness." But then it creeps up again. Well you got that hard, deep, purple layer off, but there is another layer. You forgive again and the burden is smaller, then another layer appears. It took my brother seven days of intense forgiveness. That was quick. I have found forgiveness is a process, and it can take weeks or even months. But please at least cry out to God right now; take the first step as an act of your will, forgiving those who have hurt you. Don't wait to feel warm and forgiving toward that person, you won't. Forgive out of obedience with Jesus' help–even if you don't want to.

Some people think that it is wrong to try to forgive when they don't feel like forgiving, like somehow it is phony or false. They wait for good feelings, which often never come. "When Jesus hung on the Cross in excruciating agony do you think He felt warm and fuzzy toward the people who were crucifying Him?" Obviously not. Yet He cried out: "Father, forgive them, they know not what they do." Forgiveness is an act of the will. Feelings may follow down the road, but often they do not. Doesn't matter, we must forgive. Otherwise we stay trapped in the bondage of bitterness. God wants you to be free!

Let me lead you in a simple prayer to get you started. Then you will have to do the work with the help of the Holy Spirit. Go ahead and pray this prayer.

"Heavenly Father, because you have forgiven me of all my sins and mistakes through Jesus Christ, I choose to obey your word and forgive (<u>person's name</u>)." I don't feel like forgiving, but I choose to as

an act of my will. Please help me Jesus to let go of all anger and bitterness. I release (person's name) into your hands. Thank you, Lord."

Now I want you to close your eyes and see that person standing in front of you as you *say something like this:*

> *"What you did was wrong. It really hurt me. I don't want to forgive you, but God says I must, so as an act of my will I choose to forgive you (person's name) I forgive you and I place you in God's hands. Lord help me in the future to forgive more deeply if necessarily. Thank you Jesus for your help. Amen"*

May God bless you as you take these difficult steps toward freedom in Christ!

---

[1] Celebrate Recovery is a Christ-centered recovery program founded by John Baker of Saddleback Church. The approved curriculum consists of Life's Healing Choices, Your First Step to Celebrate Recovery, and Celebrate Recovery Daily Devotional. Retrieved from www.celebraterecovery.com on 9/13/16 [2] Healing Rooms were started by John Glake in Spokane, Washington in 1914. From 1915-1920 over 10,000 miraculous healings occurred and Spokane was recognized as the healthiest city in the U.S. Cal Pierce re-opened the Healing Rooms in Spokane in 1999. We started Healing Rooms here in January, 2008. We have had hundreds of healings since that time.

Section 8

SPEAKING OR PRAYING IN TONGUES

"This heavenly language opens up a door into the Father's presence, which is the only place where we can receive deep revelations right from His mouth."
-Sunday Adalaja

Speaking in tongues is a topic that has caused much controversy. We will clear up a lot of misconceptions by looking at God's Word. Tongues are to help believers not confuse them!

Chapter 20:

The Full Spectrum of Beliefs

A very Controversial Subject

"Speaking in tongues!" That just sounds weird. Only extreme people would do something like that! What is the purpose of making strange sounds that make no sense to anyone including the one making the sounds? However, by writing a book called *Life in the Spirit*, it would be wrong not to address this confusing subject.

The first time I heard someone speaking in tongues was just a few weeks after I came to know Jesus. We had traveled south from Pacific Grove, California (where we were living), down to Big Sur about an hour away. We heard of a church that met in the Grange Hall there. We walked in and saw Blacks, Whites, Hispanics and Asians; hippies and straights of all ages, together worshipping God. There were guitars and fiddles and a key board and it was wild. I thought *Wow, this is church*? It was exciting, and I sensed the presence of God like I never had before. Remember I grew up heathen!

The funny thing was as the music became quieter, I heard people praying out loud softly in English and what I thought were foreign languages. I thought to myself, *There must be a lot of foreigners here*. But later someone explained that people were worshipping in "tongues." Someone said to me that they were speaking "mysteries to God." (See 1 Cor 14:2). I was still confused but not put off and somewhat intrigued.

Speaking or praying in tongues has caused controversy among churches and Christians and even caused a breaking of fellowship over this issue. In the 70's and 80's during the Charismatic Renewal, many from different denominations (as well as some Catholics) embraced the things of the Spirit. Many spoke in tongues which created both excitement and division. I even knew of a couple who divorced primarily over this issue. How sad. While this area is important to understand it is not essential to our salvation. It is okay to disagree on this topic without being disagreeable. I am going to share biblically as I understand it on this issue. I only ask that no matter where you stand, you will be open to what I share and check it out using the Bible to verify. This will clear up misunderstandings on many sides of this subject. The Word of God is clear on this subject and will guide you to truth.

A Motto For All

We have a motto at our church: "Unity in the essentials, liberty in the non-essentials, and love in all things." If we would all hold to this motto, people would never reason to get ticked off at each other, because of tongues–or any other non-essential issue. An example of something that is essential would be the path to salvation. A person cannot become a Christian unless they personally receive Jesus Christ for the forgiveness of their sins and follow Him as their personal Lord and Savior.

An example of a non-essential would be eschatology, or when Jesus will return? Will he come back before the 7 year period of tribulation, in the middle or after the tribulation, or some other interpretation? The Lord will come again when the Father tells Him and our holding to a certain position will not cause Him to come at that time. Agreement on this is not essential. This is a topic we can have fun discussing and even disagree with another's position without breaking fellowship. Never should we fall out of fellowship with someone over a disagreement about something that is a non-essential. That is not love, it is stupidity, and we are told to "walk in love."

So let's set this straight: Although I believe a correct understanding about tongues is extremely helpful, it is not essential. What I will be sharing may be different from what you have heard before. I did not learn this from a denomination. The Holy Spirit taught me this over several years. Let's have fun examining this topic together.

Thankfully there has recently been a more tolerant attitude between believers who speak in tongues and those who don't. In April of 2015 one of the largest denominations which has been strongly opposed to tongues, passed a resolution to accept missionaries who speak in tongues. Although they did not endorse tongues, and the resolution was not passed without fervent debate, this was a major step toward reconciliation.

Praying in the Spirit

A term often used is "praying in the Spirit." Ephesians 6:18 says: "praying always with all prayer and supplication in the Spirit." This passage is referring to spiritual warfare, where tongues become an offensive weapon against the enemy. Also, Jude 20 says: "But you, beloved, building yourselves up in your most holy faith, praying in the Holy Spirit." Now some interpret this as praying solely in tongues and not in English (or your native language). Others say it means being spiritually directed or led by the Holy Spirit in one's native language, but not tongues. I believe that both groups are right and wrong. "Praying in the Spirit" can be praying in tongues or praying in English (or native language) under the leading of the Holy Spirit. So let's not get hung up on this minor misunderstanding.

Let me make it clear that whoever has sincerely received Jesus Christ as their Lord and Savior is going to Heaven. Just because they hold different positions on tongues doesn't mean they are bad people. However, a clear view on this issue will make a Christian more effective in their walk. It can open up greater revelation from the Word, stronger empowering by the Spirit and create the opportunity to see more miracles, healings and the transformation of people's lives. It can even help in getting clear direction from the Holy Spirit.

I will use "speaking" or "praying" in tongues interchangeably. Also, for the sake of clarity, I have over-simplified the categories where people stand on this issue.

As we begin, it helps to use a spectrum of beliefs on this subject. We will start on outer extremes and move toward truth which is in the center. The further from the center, the greater the misunderstanding. I will use a spectrum of beliefs the body of Christ has on this topic.

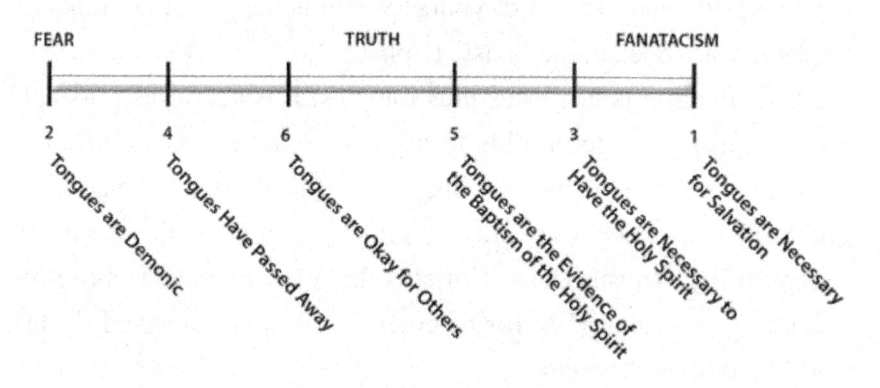

Spectrum of Belief #1: Tongues are Necessary For Salvation

Only a small group of Christians hold this position. They are sometimes called ultra-Pentecostal. They believe that tongues are essential for salvation, and if you do not speak in tongues, you are not saved. Several years ago I was traveling by air back from the East Coast to California when I started talking with the couple sitting next to me. Jesus came up in the conversation, and I asked if they were saved. They said they didn't know and responded, "We were in a church two years ago where the Gospel was presented, and we went forward. They tried to get us to speak in tongues, but we didn't, so they said we were not saved. So, we don't know. We haven't been to any church since."

I spent the next two hours on the plane convincing them that salvation was not based on tongues. I showed them scripturally that salvation had to do solely with receiving Jesus Christ as their Lord and Savior and following Him. If you ever run into someone from this small segment of Christianity you can show them Romans 10:9: "That if you confess with your mouth that Jesus is Lord and believe in your heart that God raised Him from the dead, you will be saved." Salvation comes to us through Jesus, only by the grace of God in

Jesus and our receiving it by faith: "For by grace you are saved through faith, and that not of yourselves; it is the gift of God, not of works lest anyone should boast" (Eph. 2:8).

So, salvation is not Jesus plus tongues. It is not Jesus plus baptism. Baptism is a good thing to do, but we are not saved through baptism. We are saved by receiving Jesus Christ as our personal Lord and Savior. It is not Jesus plus keeping the Torah, as the Judaizers taught. It is just Jesus. Jesus Christ is the one who gave His life for us and by receiving Him for forgiveness of sin I am saved. It has nothing to do with tongues.

As I studied this ultra-Pentecostal group's beliefs, I found that they based their position on a portion of one verse in scripture: "… and no one can say Jesus is Lord except by the Holy Spirit" (1 Cor. 12:3b). Their rationale is if you don't speak in tongues, then you don't have the Holy Spirit so you cannot honestly claim Jesus as Lord. Sadly, this is ignorance gone to seed and causes damage as it had to that couple on the airplane. I finally convinced them they had gone to a church that held a weird position on salvation. "Try other churches that preach God's Word, yet are open to the Holy Spirit. There are many out there," I told them. They promised me they would try again. Also, they left that place with a new assurance of their salvation. (1 John 5:11-13 NLT)

Notice on the spectrum I have placed "Fanaticism" on the right and "Fear" on the left. The "Fanaticism" side is when a truth is taken to an extreme where it becomes error. Now, let's look at the other side, where the position is based on fear. Sadly, I have found what people don't understand, they often reject out of fear.

Spectrum of Belief # 2: "Tongues are Demonic"

This group doesn't necessarily have any scriptural basis for their belief. Usually they have a story where a missionary heard a person praying in tongues, and it was giving glory to the devil (or something equivalent). Therefore, they say that all tongues are demonic. This is a weak supposition for sure.

Early in my Christian walk I was confused about tongues. For a couple of months I went to a small church in Princeton, New Jersey when I was attending seminary. When they heard I believed in tongues, they did a series on 'Why Tongues are of the Devil.' I knew what it was like to be influenced by the devil before I got saved, so I sensed something was wrong with their stance and the teaching made me even more confused. They were in fear. This was during the height of the Charismatic Renewal, and they seemed afraid of those "overly emotional" Christians. The three part series was to set me and others straight. I began to pray for truth and remembered seeing the scripture in my Bible: "Therefore, brethren, desire earnestly to prophesy, and do not forbid to speak with tongues" (1 Cor. 14:39). They had taken an extreme position out of fear that was far from the truth. Even as a fairly new Christian, I knew their position was off. Thank God for the revealing light from His Word!

So now that we have dealt with the extremes, let's move closer to the truth. By the way, these believers who are wrong in their positions are still saved, yet sadly they misunderstood something that could make them more effective on this earth.

Spectrum of Belief # 3: "Tongues are necessary to have the Holy Spirit."

If you will notice, we are moving closer to truth on the spectrum. This group says that you can be saved without tongues, but they believe you don't have the Holy Spirit unless you speak in tongues. What's wrong with this position? First of all, when you received Jesus, you got the whole package. Because the barrier of sin was broken, you moved into a more intimate relationship with God. Romans 8:15b refers to our salvation by saying "…but you received the Spirit of adoption by whom we cry out, 'Abba, Father'." The Holy Spirit came to inhabit you immediately at that point when you received Jesus. This was not dependent upon your speaking in tongues.

A scripture you could use to help someone caught in this error is: "Or do you not know that your body is the temple of the Holy Spirit Who is in you, whom you have from God, and you are not your own?" (1 Cor.6:19 NIV). It doesn't say, we are the temple of the Holy Spirit if we "speak in tongues." So scripture is addressing believers, and it says that we (believers) are all collectively the temple of the Holy Spirit. The Holy Spirit dwells in us instead of in the Holy of Holies. When Jesus came into your life so did the Holy Spirit! I am not saying that you can't have deeper ongoing experiences with the Holy Spirit because you can. There is a further empowering of the Holy Spirit available to you.

This empowering or (baptism of the Holy Spirit) can happen simultaneously when you are saved, but oftentimes it happens subsequent to salvation. When the Holy Spirit comes to live in us at the moment of salvation, He begins producing the fruit of the Spirit in us. Yet fruit is not produced overnight. It is a long process of the inner working of the Holy Spirit in us. "But the fruit of the Spirit is love, joy, peace, patience, kindness, goodness, faithfulness, gentleness, self-control" (Gal. 5:22-23a) This process is called sanctification, or becoming more like Jesus.

Spectrum of Belief No. 4: Tongues have passed away." (Cessationism)

As we move closer to the truth, this group makes up a large segment of "Evangelical" Christianity. Cessationism is the belief that the Gifts of the Spirit passed away after the early church and New Testament were established. Often churches do not explain their position; they just refuse to acknowledge or allow any of the gifts to operate, rejecting the supernatural aspects of the Holy Spirit (especially "speaking in tongues.")

I have already addressed the fallacy of Cessationism as a theological position in section 4. These evangelical cessationist churches are in many cases very good churches. They are leading people to Christ and are usually diligent with discipleship, but denying the fullness of the Holy Spirit's empowering. While they enjoy much fruitfulness, they miss out on the power God longs for them to explore.

A few years ago there was a Chinese underground pastor who traveled the U.S. visiting many churches for 8 months. I watched an interview where he was asked: "After viewing the American church for many months and experiencing their services and community, what would you have to comment?" He waited for several seconds and then said words I will never forget.

"I am amazed at how much the American church has been able to accomplish without the power and presence of the Holy Spirit." Wow, what a powerful observation from a man who has pastored for years in a nation that persecutes true Christianity.

Let us move to the other side of the spectrum.

Spectrum of Belief # 5: "Tongues are the Evidence of the Baptism of the Holy Spirit"

The Azusa Street Revival

On April 9th, 1906 a group of primarily African Americans moved into an abandoned livery stable on Azusa Street in Los Angeles, California. The meetings, headed by William J. Seymour, had grown and word began to spread quickly about this outpouring of the Holy Spirit. From 1906 until 1908, this Spirit-led movement hosted thousands of people from around the world. There were many manifestations from fire on the roof to a thick shining haze inside (known as the "*shekinah* glory"). The fire department was even called on several occasions. There were many miraculous healings and several young children saw powerful visions. Many came to know Christ. There were countless prophecies both personal and for the nation, but the Azusa Street Revival was best known for people being "Baptized in the Holy Spirit with the evidence of speaking in tongues."

William J. Seymour would often preach from Acts 2:4: *And they were all filled with the Holy Spirit and began to speak with other tongues, as the Spirit gave them utterance*. This New Testament phenomenon spread far beyond the crowds of Azusa Street circling the globe. Many places in the U.S., Africa, Europe, South America, Australia and beyond experienced this phenomenon. People would crowd in for services daily often standing rows deep outside the building, and then they would take this phenomenon back to their home towns.

Another amazing fact about this revival was the total breakdown of all social, economic, and racial barriers. At a time of intense prejudices and strict social dividing lines, many believe this was the first truly integrated church in the United States. All barriers fell under the anointing of the Holy Spirit. The very wealthy mingled with the very poor. Those of high social standing mixed comfortably with those who had no social status. One of the greatest miracles was the mingling of all races: African American, Hispanics, Whites, Asians, Native Americans and other ethnic backgrounds blended together as this family of God pursued the move of the Holy Spirit and His presence.

The concept of the "baptism of the Holy Spirit" was not a new one. Charles Finney, the famous evangelist of the early 1800's had shared his story of this "baptism" which changed his life. He wrote about this experience which made him effective in the Lord's work."

D.L. Moody

D.L. Moody, who made his mark as one of the greatest evangelist in the second half of the nineteenth century, also talked about the importance of the "baptism of the Holy Spirit." He had been a shoe salesman with a fifth grade education turned Sunday school teacher. His Sunday school in Chicago grew during this time of the Industrial Revolution. Sadly his church, Sunday school, and home all went up in smoke in the "Great Chicago Fire", October 8, 1871.

Earlier that year, two elderly ladies named Annie Cook and Mrs. Snow approached D.L., emphasizing his need for the "empowering of the Spirit." Although somewhat irked, he allowed them to pray for him. Broken and not sure of his direction, he was desperately seeking the Holy Spirit. Ironically it would be 10 weeks after the Chicago fire, walking down Wall Street in New York City that the Holy Spirit would change his life. In D.L. Moody's own words: "*I was crying all the time that God would fill me with His Spirit. Well, one day, in the city of New York – oh what a day – I cannot describe it, I seldom refer to it; it is almost too sacred an experience to name. I can only say that God revealed Himself to me, and I had such an experience of His love that I had to ask Him to stay His hand. I went to preaching again. The sermons were no different; I did not present any new truths and yet hundreds were converted. I would not now be placed back where I was before that blessed experience, if you should give me the world.*" (*The Helper,* Catherine Marshall pp 25-26)

After the experience of the "baptism of the Holy Spirit," Moody became famous, preaching all over the world leading thousands to Christ. In the late 1800's he held conferences where people would go out to a hill (in Northfield, Massachusetts) to wait until receiving this empowerment. But Moody never really talked about speaking in tongues. Then in the early 1900s, belief that speaking in tongues was the evidence of the baptism in the Holy Spirit burst on the scene.

As already mentioned the "Azusa Street Revival" (1906 – 1908), was the primary force launching the Pentecostal Movement which birthed such denominations as the Assemblies of God, Church of God and others. They all had this key doctrine in common. They promoted the baptism of the Holy Spirit with the evidence of speaking in tongues." Pentecostals in the first half of the twentieth century were often looked down upon and experienced ridicule and persecution for their beliefs. Although they brought a renewed interest in the Holy Spirit, there were aspects of their denominational positions that were not edifying. Legalism began to take a strong hold. Rigid rules replaced freedom and motivation by the Spirit. Also, the doctrine that "tongues" was the sole evidence of the baptism of the Holy Spirit was incorrect.

The Charismatic Movement

Starting in the late 1960's and continuing deep into the 1980's, the Charismatic Renewal hit the U.S. and countries around the world. The position that speaking in tongues was the evidence required for having received the baptism in the Holy Spirit was now being adopted by most Charismatic's from mainline denominations. Even though much renewal and good came from this revival, there was error as well. The primary error was linking two separate experiences into one: The "baptism of the Holy Spirit" and "Speaking in Tongues" as having to occur simultaneously. These are two different experiences that can happen at the same time but often do not. Sadly, many believed the error that if a person didn't speak in tongues they did not have the baptism (or empowering) of the Holy Spirit. This is a false understanding that many still hold today.

Billy Graham, the great evangelist of the twentieth century, who probably led more people to Christ than anyone during his time–was baptized in the Holy Spirit while in Wales as mentioned earlier. He seldom talked about how it changed his life and was responsible for his incredible success as an evangelist. Because he grew up in a denomination that rejected tongues, to our knowledge he didn't speak in tongues. I believe it would be very hard to argue that Billy Graham was not "baptized" (empowered) by the Holy Spirit. Billy definitely received the power talked about in Acts 1:8. The same may be said of D.L. Moody and Charles Finney. Therefore speaking in tongues can be an <u>evidence</u> but cannot be <u>the only</u> evidence of the baptism of the Holy Spirit. (See section three for more.)

Examining Biblically

The baptism of the Holy Spirit and speaking in tongues are two separate experiences that can happen at the same time, but often they do not. There are six times in the book of Acts where it actually mentions people who were baptized in the Holy Spirit, but only three of those times mention tongues. The other three say nothing about tongues. You can't make a solid doctrine out of two occurrences that happened simultaneously only 50% of the time in the book of Acts. You may look these up if you choose. The three that mention tongues are:

- Acts 2:4;
- Acts 10:44-46
- Acts 19:6.

The three which do not mention tongues are:

- Acts 4:31
- Acts 8:17
- Acts 9:17-18. (Note: Paul did later speak in tongues but in this reference, there is no mention of it in his initial baptism of the Holy Spirit.)

Remember the story of the church in Big Sur, California? The one where I thought there were foreigners since I knew nothing about speaking in tongues? Well, I had only been saved a few weeks. At this church they would pray by turning around and kneeling by their chairs. As people prayed I turned around and kneeled also. All of a sudden, there were people around me laying hands on me and I started speaking in tongues. They said, "You got it, you got it."

I thought *Got what*?

I figured whatever I had gotten was good because they were all excited. They said, "You got the baptism of the Holy Spirit."

I said, "I do?" I didn't know what that meant.

Clearing up Confusion

They told me since I spoke in tongues that I had received the baptism of the Holy Spirit. The problem was I experienced no empowering at all, I simply spoke in tongues. So I was confused. I thought the reason for speaking in tongues was so if anyone asked me if I had received "the baptism," I could say "Yes".

I saw no reason to speak in tongues after that. I didn't speak in tongues for several years until the Holy Spirit revealed biblically to me the purpose of tongues. Then I began to use this as a powerful way of praying (I will explain that purpose a little further on). Ironically, about six months later, I did experience the baptism of the Holy Spirit which definitely empowered me to be a stronger believer, increased my hunger for His Word and His presence, and made me more effective in His Kingdom.

Jesus made it clear the purpose of the baptism of the Holy Spirit would empower us to have a greater impact on others. "*But you shall receive power when the Holy Spirit has come upon you; and you shall be <u>witnesses to</u> <u>Me</u> in Jerusalem, and in all Judea and Samaria, and to the end of the earth.*" (Acts 1:8)

The baptism of the Holy Spirit empowers each one of us beyond our natural ability or faculties, and it is available to every believer. Sometimes this empowering comes very subtly and other times dramatically. It may come in stages.

There are some who believe this empowering can only happen once, but Ephesians 5:18-19 refutes that. "And do not be drunk with wine, in which is dissipation; but be filled with the Spirit, speaking to one another in psalms and hymns and spiritual songs, singing and making melody in your heart to the Lord" (Eph. 5:18-19). The phrase "be filled" is in the present, progressive tense in the original language. Thus, this would literally read "be, being filled, on an ongoing basis."

The Amplified Bible translates this: "ever be filled and stimulated." In other words, it is not a onetime filling where you pull up to the Heavenly gas tank and get filled. Then God says "Well, good luck… hope you can get through the rest of your life on that one filling!" No, the Holy Spirit wants to fill you over and over again. This can happen while worshipping, reading His word, praying with other believers, or taking a walk in the woods, etc. Don't ever put the Holy Spirit in a box.

The hungrier and thirstier you are for that infilling, the greater the probability of being filled. People who are not hungry for food will probably not eat. The same is true of the Holy Spirit. "Blessed are those who hunger and thirst for righteousness, For they shall be filled." (Matt. 5:6 NKJV) Going after righteousness (right standing) with God means hungering for a deeper relationship with God, Jesus and the Holy Spirit.

During the Charismatic Renewal, many times pride would accompany those who spoke in tongues. They could boast they had the "baptism of the Holy Spirit" evidenced by speaking in tongues while others did not. God does not have an "in" crowd or an "out" crowd. The baptism of the Holy Spirit and tongues are available to all believers, not just a special few. Everybody is in His "in" crowd.

Spectrum of Belief # 6. Tongues are Okay for Others

This group is getting closer to the truth. They say it is okay for other people to speak in tongues, but it is probably not for them. They may think, "If God forces me, then maybe I will speak in tongues." But that will never happen because God won't make you. You will never be coerced, but you have to be willing. In fact it helps if you truley desire to speak in tongues or flow in the gifts of the Spirit. "But earnestly desire the best gifts. And yet I will show you a more excellent way." (1 Cor 12:31) "Earnestly desire" is the Greek word "*zeloo*" which means to burn with a white, hot fervor. The best gift is always the gift that is most necessary at that time. When I go into a hospital room and somebody is dying of cancer, probably the gift of prophecy is not the best gift for that situation. The gifts of healing, miracles, and faith would be the best for the situation.

In the next chapter we will move to the middle of the spectrum where we find the truth.

Chapter 21:

Exploring the Mystery

What is the Purpose of Speaking or Praying in Tongues?

Many churches in the U.S. do not explain the purpose of tongues. Those who do not see the relevance of tongues for today (Cessasionists), have no reason to teach on it. Other more seeker sensitive churches are concerned they might offend or confuse unbelievers, so even though their doctrinal position may accept the gifts of the Holy Spirit as relevant for today, they too steer clear of tongues. Then there are some churches which are just plain ignorant on this topic. So if much of the mainstream evangelical church either does not believe in or does not teach on tongues, how can it be that important? What is the purpose of speaking or praying in tongues?

To start with, speaking in tongues is different than the gift of tongues. This one fact often helps clear up a lot of initial confusion. This confusion first showed up in the Corinthian church. People would just blurt out in tongues (their prayer language), in the service and there would be no interpretation following because it wasn't the "gift of tongues" in operation. Paul said, "I thank God I speak in tongues more than you all." (He must have lived in southern Jerusalem!) But, in the church I would rather speak five words in my native language than 10,000 words in tongues" (1 Cor. 14:18). Why? Because speaking in tongues as a prayer language is not edifying to a group of people, it only builds up the faith of the individual (Jude 1:20). The gift of tongues is edifying to the body of Christ only if it is followed by the gift of interpretation of tongues. So there was confusion and chaos in the Corinthian church. He was trying to teach them, and thank God he did because it brings clarity to us today.

The gifts are always to help other people, not ourselves (1 Cor 12:7 NLT). Speaking or praying in tongues is to help us personally and not someone else. "He who speaks in a tongue edifies himself, but he who prophesies edifies the church." (2 Cor. 14:4 NKJV) So, my prayer language is used to edify myself. The gift of tongues is to help others when followed by the gift of interpretation of tongues.

Build Up Your Human Spirit

The purpose of praying or speaking in tongues is to build ourselves up! When I pray in tongues I am speaking mysteries to God (1 Corinthians 14:2). I don't understand what I am saying, but the Holy Spirit is praying through my human spirit. This in turn builds up my human spirit. When your human spirit is built up, you become stronger in the Lord. You become more receptive to the Holy Spirit and receive greater impartation, revelation, and gifting for service. You receive greater revelation from God's Word because you are more spiritually attuned. You are able to pray for others with a greater leading of the Spirit and you receive clearer direction from the Holy Spirit; so tongues is very helpful.

What does it mean to be built up in our human spirit? We are made in the image of God. He is one God in three parts: Father, Son, and Holy Spirit. We are also one person in three parts: (human) spirit, soul, and body. (1 Thess. 5:23 NIV)

Our body is the earth suit we live in. We have a soul which is made up of our mind, emotions and will. And we are a human spirit. That is the part of us that comes alive when we are "born again." When you received Jesus your human spirit came alive to God. The Holy Spirit came to inhabit your human spirit. That is why when your spirit is built up it affects your entire being and makes you more empowered to follow the Holy Spirit's leading.

When I received Christ I told God, "I deeply need all the help You can give me." So, I was open to whatever God had for me. I read in 1 Corinthians that tongues is to "build myself up." So now, when I am headed to pray for somebody who is dying of cancer, I am praying in tongues much of the way. This builds me up so I am not overwhelmed by my emotions and therefore better able to pray a Spirit-led prayer, (in English), and release healing and comfort to that person. I usually try to "build myself up in my most Holy faith" (Jude 20), before I go in to pray or minister. I try to be receptive to the Holy Spirit at all times because I know how powerless and ineffective I am in my own self. Effectiveness comes through Him!

Recently, a young couple called me and told me that their 8 month old child was diagnosed with a brain tumor and asked if I could come and pray for the child. Immediately, my emotions went bonkers. I felt deeply for this helpless, beautiful little boy. I began lifting this child before the Lord, praying in tongues privately. The longer I prayed, the more I felt my emotions calm down and God's presence encompass me. When I went to pray for the child, I sensed a strong anointing and really felt internally that this child would be healed.

Every now and then my emotions of pity and fear for the child would rise up, but I would pray quietly in tongues and it would dissipate.

Two weeks later we got the news. The baby was completely healed – no brain tumor, it had vanished! Many prayers had gone up for this baby and God answered our cry. Spirit led praying is powerful.

In the Bible, God spoke through "Balaam's ass" (Numbers 22:28 KJV). That should give us all encouragement. If He can use a donkey, I know He can use us! God is looking for our availability even more than our ability. When we are puffed up with our own giftedness, it hinders us from being able to operate in the power of the Holy Spirit and achieve the results He desires. I know that tongues have helped me in a variety of ways, and it can help you!

Reasons People Don't Speak in Tongues

There are many reasons why people don't speak in tongues. The primary one is false teaching such as believing that tongues have passed away and are no longer valid for today. If a person doesn't believe tongues are relevant for today or see a purpose in the practice, they won't speak in tongues.

Another reason is believing tongues are only for special people following a special experience. I have encountered several people who think speaking in tongues is a valid experience, but they are not special enough. Jesus debunks this myth.

"And these signs will follow those who believe: In My name they will cast out demons; they will speak with new tongues" (Mark 16:17).

The Bible doesn't say those who are special or have a special experience (baptized in the Holy Spirit) will speak with new tongues. It says those who believe. According to Jesus being a believer is the only prerequisite for speaking in tongues!

A third reason is because they can be overly self-conscious. Some may be concerned they may not be doing it right, or they may have heard others with really impressive sounding tongues and theirs is just a few repeated syllables. I encourage people who feel like this to go off alone, away from all people, and go ahead and pray in tongues. This often helps them to break through their self consciousness.

The Greatest Hindrance

Over the last several years I have found the greatest hindrance to speaking in tongues is the rejection of this phenomenon by the analytical mind in people. The more analytical a person is, the harder it is for them to break through into tongues. I also have found that overly analytical people receive greater help from tongues because it brings that part of the brain under the dominion of the human spirit by the Holy Spirit. People who have a tendency to experience the "paralysis of over analysis" are greatly helped when they allow the power of God to supercede their reasoning.

A scripture that brings clarity to an analytical person is this: "For if I pray in a tongue, my spirit prays, but my understanding (mind) is unfruitful" (1 Cor. 14:14). In other words the mind is not involved in tongues. It doesn't understand what is being said. It is unable to validate what is actually tongues or not. The mind will automatically reject tongues because it is not filtered through understanding. This can be very frustrating to the analytical person. Tongues sound like gibberish and makes no sense. This is by God's design! The Holy Spirit is bypassing the intellect and going right to the human spirit which is doing the praying.

I am somewhat analytical, and I had a hard time praying in tongues even after I saw its validity. I would time myself for five minutes. I would think, *Time's up!* Then I would check my watch and only 45 seconds had ticked off! Why? Because my analytical mind was fighting me! After a few months of praying in tongues, my mind stopped fighting it. Now I pray in tongues even when I'm not thinking about it. I believe Paul had praying tongues in mind when he wrote "pray without ceasing" (1 Thessalonians 5:17). When you pray through your intellect, your mind gets tired. But praying in tongues is different because the Holy Spirit is praying through your human spirit. You can go on and on indefinitely.

Some people say, "But I don't understand what I am praying." That is true because you are praying through your human spirit by the Holy Spirit. It is supposed to be beyond your intellectual comprehension. Other people say, "Well, shouldn't this be a known language?" Paul didn't think so, he said "If I speak in the tongue of men or <u>angels</u>" (1 Cor. 13:1) There is no Rosetta Stone course available for people to learn the tongue of angels! Also, if it had to be a known tongue then people would be "translating" rather than operating in the gift of "interpretation." If tongues had to be a known language, then it wouldn't be "speaking mysteries to God." (1 Cor. 14:2)

Several years ago I was praying for an extremely cerebral young guy who had a scholarship from Julliard School of Music. He was very analytical, and he wanted to speak in tongues. I prayed for him and nothing happened. I saw this picture of his cerebrum attached to a microscope looking down on his tongue not allowing anything to come out. When I described what I saw, he said that was exactly how it felt. He said that he desired to speak in tongues so badly, but he couldn't. He felt like something was trapped.

He called me the next day excited saying that he woke up in the middle of the night speaking in tongues! He was able to do this because in the middle of the night his conscious mind let go. He told me what freed him from his over analysis was speaking in tongues. He explained that it empowered him to allow his gifting in music to now be used to lead other people in worship. It helped him move beyond his perfectionism and fear of failure. When I last talked with him he was leading worship at a church in Arizona. What a blessing!

The Holy Spirit Doesn't Take Over Your Will

I have encountered people who expect the Holy Spirit to move their tongue for them, and make sounds come out. So, they are waiting and waiting...and waiting for something to happen. They say "Okay, I want to speak in tongues, but nothing is happening." In all my years of speaking in tongues, I have never had an experience where I was speaking English when suddenly strange sounds started coming out of my mouth. That is not going to happen. So, if you are waiting for the Holy Spirit to move your tongue, Jesus will return before that happens. You have to do the speaking or praying in tongues just like you have to do it when praying in English.

The scripture for this was on the day of Pentecost. "And they were all filled with the Holy Spirit and (they) began to speak with other tongues, as the Spirit gave them utterance" (Acts 2:4). Now, who did the speaking? They had to do the speaking and they did. In the original Greek, this verse was written in the third person plural. Literally it says, they were all filled with the Holy Spirit and they began to speak with other tongues. But, the translators don't put the word "they" in twice, it is understood. So for you to speak in tongues, you have to do the speaking.

A Word To The Skeptical

An article published November 7, 2006 in the *New York Times* entitled "*A* Neuroscientific look at Speaking in Tongues" by Benedict Carey detailed some startling scientific discoveries about speaking in tongues. Researchers at the University of Pennsylvania took brain images of five women while they spoke in tongues and found that their frontal lobes – the thinking, willful part of the brain through which people control what they do – were relatively quiet, as were the language centers. On the other hand, the regions involved in maintaining sub-consciousness were very active. The women were not in blind trances, and it was unclear which region was driving the behavior." This supports that "speaking in tongues" goes beyond the intellectual centers of the brain. This research demonstrates a power that transcends the logical portions of the brain.

Contrary to what may be a common perception, studies suggest that people who speak in tongues rarely suffer from mental problems. A recent study of nearly 1,000 Christians in England found that "those who engaged in this practice were more emotionally stable than those who did not." The new findings contrasted sharply with images taken of other spiritually inspired mental states like meditation, which is often a highly focused mental exercise, activating the frontal lobes.

The scans also showed a dip in the activity of a region called the left caudate. "The findings from the frontal lobes are very clear, and make sense, but the caudate is usually active when you have positive effect, pleasure, or positive emotions," said Dr. James A. Coan, a psychologist at the University of Virginia. "The caudate area is also involved in motor and emotional control."

The personal benefits I have found in speaking in tongues are many. It increases my ability to receive from God whether it is peace, direction, empowering, or greater revelation from the Word or my circumstances. At times I have battled anxiety, and I have found that speaking or praying in tongues is very helpful in lessening that anxiety to bring a peace. I usually sense a closer connection with the Holy Spirit.

The only reference I can find in the Old Testament to tongues seems to be referring to a future time, but mentions rest and refreshing. "For with stammering lips and another tongue He will speak to this people to whom He said, 'This is the rest with which you may cause the body to rest, And this is the refreshing" (Isa. 28:11-12). This seems to be born out scientifically as well. Notice how it seems to bypass the analytical, cognitive part of the brain. But let's move on so you can speak in tongues or become more fluent in tongues.

The Only Prerequisite for Speaking in Tongues

All that is required to be able to speak in tongues is being a believer in Jesus (Mark 16:17). You don't have to have a special experience, be a pastor, a missionary or an evangelist. Speaking in tongues can be helpful to all areas of your life and is not just for church activities. As a believer it is available to you, but you don't have to do it. You will still go to heaven and you can still have an impact here. But why turn it down? Go for it!

This is my prayer for you:

"Heavenly Father, I want to praise You that You did not leave us powerless. I thank you, Jesus, that before You left earth You said we would be better off when the Holy Spirit came, and He would be our comforter, advocate, helper and empowerer. You said the Holy Spirit would be many things to us, and I am so grateful for You, Holy Spirit. Lord, we thank You they will speak in new tongues. It may not make

sense to their natural mind, but You will be edifying them andbuilding them up in their spirit. In Jesus' name, amen."

Now pray this prayer:

"Heavenly Father, I thank You that Jesus said, 'Those who believe would speak with new tongues.' I am a believer now and therefore I believe I will speak in tongues as the Spirit gives me utterance. Thank You Father, in Jesus' name!"

Right where you are, go ahead and close your eyes, focus on God and speak in tongues. Remember you are speaking "mysteries to God" which you don't understand. Your mind will fight you, but let yourself explore this new adventure. Don't be discouraged if it doesn't happen immediately, don't give up. Remember you have to do the speaking. May God bless you!

Section 9

THE COMFORTING ROLE OF THE HOLY SPIRIT

"How sweet the name of Jesus sounds, in a believer's ear!
The (Holy) Spirit soothes our sorrows,
heals our wounds, and drives away our fear."
-John Newton

Before Jesus was crucified, He talked to his disciples about the Holy Spirit being our "comforter." Thank God, He is still comforting people today in our fallen world.

Chapter 22:

The Comforter

Living in a fallen world, life can often take a difficult, unexpected turn. Let's examine the essential role of the Holy Spirit as the **comforter**. "Then the churches throughout all Judea, Galilee, and Samaria had peace and were edified. And walking in the fear of the Lord and in the comfort of the Holy Spirit, they were multiplied." (Acts 9:31) With the persecution and personal struggles in the early days of the church, the Holy Spirit played a significant role.

Somebody lied to me when I first became a Christian. They said that once I had became a believer, I wouldn't go through any more struggles. Sad to say I have had plenty of struggles, but the good news is that I had someone to go through them with me: the Holy Spirit! Jesus tried to warn his disciples (and us) about this just before He went to the cross: "I have told you all this so that you may have peace in me. Here on earth you will have many trials and sorrows. But take heart, because I have overcome the world" (John 16:33 NLT). We don't often talk about "the Comforter," but it is one of His most important roles."

I am sure you could tell me of horrendous struggles you have gone through. One of mine occurred six years into pastoring my first church where we were having a mini-revival. God was showing up powerfully in the services and during the week. There were people getting healed, delivered and saved every week, and the presence of the Holy Spirit was tangible. The head bartender of the largest bar in town got saved and asked me if he should stop tending the bar. I said, "No way, you have a more powerful ministry than I do!" A young girl was set free of heroin with no withdrawal! There was a growing cult there called "The Way," that was totally dissolved as a result of intercessory prayer. We saw God literally transform the town. There are still people there who talk about the outpouring of the Holy Spirit from 1980 to 1984. I was riding a wave of the Spirit and having a great time.

In my sixth year in Grand Lake, I felt a burden for Asia and that we were to move there to minister. I spent three weeks in China checking it out and learning the language. I spent a week in Taiwan and then went to Hong Kong for another week. There I stayed at an old British Army Hospital owned by Youth With A Mission. It was a beautiful place on a hill overlooking the city of Hong Kong. I felt God was calling me to go with YWAM and to be leading teams into many Asian countries. I was very excited about it and was accepted into the program.

When I came back to Grand Lake, my wife, who had stayed home with our two young children, was acting strange. I knew something was wrong and asked her what was going on. She said that she had fallen in love with another man. She said that she still loved me but was also in love with someone else. I was devastated. For the next several months, she went back and forth between the two of us. Finally, I told her this was not fair to me, to her, to the children or to the church. So a few days later she came to me and said that she was not only leaving me, but was also leaving the kids. I was overwhelmed. I never thought this could happen. She was a great mom and this was unthinkable.

I never imagined I would go through anything like this. I had been fully committed to the marriage. At times, perhaps I was over committed to the ministry, but I never sought out other women The church was gracious wanting me to stay on as their pastor. I asked God what I should do, and he told me to move to Greeley, Colorado. I didn't know many people there, but I had raised someone up to take my place as pastor, so I left for Greeley. A missionary came, and drove everything we had in a U-Haul. My two young children and our golden retriever scrunched into my VW station wagon and off we went. I arrived with no wife, no money and no job, only a Word from the Lord! I was holding on to Jesus by a thread!

Why Greeley, Colorado you might ask? I asked the same question. I had been there once before and remembered a strong smell that came from the many cattle yards there. I figured maybe God wanted me to move there because it smelled the way I felt!

I do want to say that during that time the Lord was so close. The Holy Spirit really became an incredible "comfort" to me. One morning I woke up so depressed, I didn't think I could go on or even get out of bed. Hands literally lifted me off the bed. I stood there in my BVD's! I don't know if it was Jesus' hands, angelic hands, or the Holy Spirit, but deep down I knew I was going to make it. I really learned that the Comforter was someone who would come to me and help me in my times of deepest need.

"And I will ask the Father, and He will give you another Comforter (Counselor, Helper, Intercessor, Advocate, Strengthener, and Standby), that He may remain with you forever – Peace I leave

with you. My (own) peace I now give and bequeath to you. Not as the world gives do I give to you. Do not let your hearts be troubled, neither let them be afraid. (Stop allowing yourselves to be agitated and disturbed, and do not permit yourselves to be fearful and intimidated and cowardly and unsettled.)"
- John 14:16, 27 AMP

It is important you realize this truth so you can call on Him when you are in trouble. The Holy Spirit came to me constantly during that difficult time, and I experienced a greater closeness than I had ever experienced before. It was an amazing time. I prayed my wife would come back. In fact, I prayed for over a year. I didn't date or even want to; I was so beat up inside. During that time, I had some wonderful friends who came alongside me. But I also learned a very hard lesson. I discovered that some of the people I thought were my friends were not there for me during my divorce. They loved me when I was pastoring an on fire church, but not now that I was divorced. They seemed to avoid or ignore me. Maybe they were just uncomfortable, but they were no longer there for me. Some people I didn't think were necessarily my friends surprised me; they were really there for me and uplifted me. I decided that from now on I was going to be authentic. I would build relationships with people that were very real and transparent. When you think a certain person is your friend and all of a sudden they treat you like you have the plague, that's painful!

I thank God the "Comforter" was very close to me at that time. When I look back, even though it was a very, very hard time, I am glad the Holy Spirit walked me through it and I am grateful for the lessons I learned. It was during that time that I met Yvonne, and we have been married now for over 30 years. She was single, and came along just in the nick of time, helping me to raise my children.. I am so very thankful for her. She was the second comforter to come into my life. I would not be where I am today without her and the Holy Spirit's help!

Something else the Holy Spirit helped with was the anger, resentment and bitterness I felt toward my ex-wife. She had moved on and married the man she had fallen in love with. It took a few years but gradually the Holy Spirit helped me to forgive her from my heart. Thankfully my ex-wife re-established good relationships with the children. When 9-11 happened she wrote me a long letter asking forgiveness for the mistake she had made. I told her that I had forgiven her years before and asked forgiveness for my failings. We have had a civil relationship because of the children and now grandchildren. We have even spent Thanksgivings together with the entire family, and I have enjoyed it. God restores!

Let me say if you have been wounded by someone recently or even years ago and you still feel anger and resentment, you must let it go. It will only mess you up, and your relationship with God will suffer. "Put away anger, wrath, evil speaking and bitterness, be kind and tender hearted, forgiving one another, just as God in Christ has forgiven you" (Eph. 4:31). The Holy Spirit will help you to let go. If you're struggling, take a step of faith as an act of your will: forgive! You may not feel like it which is okay; do it anyway. Go back and pray the prayer on forgiveness at the end of Section # 7. Be free my brother and sister in Jesus Name!

Depend on the Holy Spirit in Weakness and Struggle

When we look at the Apostle Paul's life, he went through some very difficult times. He records it like this:

Five different times the Jewish leaders gave me thirty-nine lashes. Three times I was beaten with rods. Once I was stoned. Three times I was shipwrecked. Once I spent a whole night and a day adrift at sea. I have traveled on many long journeys. I have faced danger from rivers and from robbers. I have faced danger from my own people, the Jews, as well as from the Gentiles. I have faced danger in the cities, in the deserts, and on the seas. And I have faced danger from men who claim to be believers but are not. I have worked hard and long, enduring many sleepless nights. I have been hungry and thirsty and have often gone without food. I have shivered in the cold, without enough clothing to keep me warm. Then, besides all this, I have the daily burden of my concern for all the churches. Who is weak without my feeling that weakness? Who is led astray, and I do not burn with anger? If I must boast, I would rather boast about the things that show how weak I am."

- (2 Cor. 11:23b-30 NLT)

He went through so many struggles… after his encounter with Jesus. Before that he was the Jewish superstar of the day, elevated in everyone's eyes, and even chosen to stop the "cult" of Christianity. He was wined and dined as a celebrity. But then after meeting Jesus on the Damascus Road, things changed dramatically. If his struggles weren't enough, often his closest friends would desert him when he needed them the most. Many theologians believe his wife left him as well since he had been on the Sanhedrin where one had to be married. What did he learn? To depend upon the Holy Spirit in human weakness and struggle! When we are weak and are struggling, there is somebody there who will strengthen us and that somebody is the Holy Spirit!

Paul learned much about the comfort of the Holy Spirit in trials. He came to the conclusion that suffering persecution and satanic attacks were worth it because he gained so much insight and power from the Holy Spirit in his weakness. He writes: "That is why I take pleasure in my weaknesses and in the insults, hardships, persecutions, and troubles that I suffer for Christ. For when I am weak, then I am strong" (2 Cor. 12:10 NLT). The Amplified Bible says:"...for when I am weak (in human strength) then I am (truly) strong (able, powerful in divine strength)."

This is an important principle. Growing up I didn't feel weak. I was Captain of the wrestling team in high school and part of a championship football team. I went on to play football, rugby and wrestle in college. I coached wrestling, football and rugby when I graduated. But it was later in my times of real emotional weakness that I came to discover His <u>divine</u> strength.

My best friend in seminary was a man named Bill Gaskell. He is a Presbyterian Pastor in Cherry Hill, New Jersey. We had both been hippies and Zen Buddhists before we became Christians, so we really hit it off. We owned a painting company together in seminary. He called me a few years ago telling me how he found his 22 year old son on the couch in his basement with a needle hanging from his arm. His son had overdosed on drugs. His wife came down and started screaming. They called 911, but he had already died. Bill prayed his son would come back to life, but he didn't. He said it was by far the hardest thing anyone can go through. He wrote a book called, *Gold Mining in the Pit of Sorrow.*

That was a horrific time for him and his wife. We spent some time praying together, when I was back there. Losing a child is one of the hardest things you can ever face. But, he said, out of that he learned so much, and the Holy Spirit was such a comfort to him. Since then he and his wife have been able to comfort countless people that have lost children. The Holy Spirit can bring good out of the saddest of tragedies.

Another couple we are very close to lost their only son to suicide. We met them at Denver International Airport as they fell into our arms sobbing. All we could do was pray with them and hug them. They have struggled but are slowly coming through this terrible trial. Thank God for the Holy Spirit who comforts us in our darkest trials, and thank God for caring believers who will come along side of us in deepest times of need!

Trials Bring Opportunity

When you go through serious trials, it provides opportunities for you later, to bring comfort to others in those same areas. So many people have called me over the years asking me to pray for them because a spouse left. I don't know how some of these people found out about my situation, but I have received calls in the middle of the night. I have been able to minister to them because I have been there and I can empathize and understand their pain. That is one reason we have such a heart for single parents in our present church, because I was one. That is why we have so many classes to strengthen marriages, because I don't want anyone to have to go through what I went through. But, we also have Divorce Recovery when someone goes through a divorce because we want to be there for them. We also have a seminar for blended families.

Sometimes the church in general isn't there for people going through these kind of struggles, and I think it is wrong. Thank God for the Holy Spirit, He models for us what it looks like to bring comfort. As He leads us, we become comforters to others by His compassion and power. "He comforts us in all our troubles so that we can comfort others. When they are troubled, we will be able to give them the same comfort God had given us" (2 Corinthians 1:4 NLT). This is often how ministries are birthed.

Jesus went through amazing struggles. Basically, his disciples failed him in his hour of need. Remember they fell asleep. They weren't there for him. The Heavenly Father even turned away from Jesus when He took on the sins of the world, causing Him to cry out: "Father, why have You forsaken me?" He experienced rejection, abandonment and pain. Whatever hardship we may have experienced, (in childhood, later in your life, or maybe even now) we must allow the Holy Spirit to come in and bring healing. This is a process not an instantaneous moment.

I really needed those few people who really loved me despite the fact I was no longer "Pastor" JR from an exciting revival church. During this time, I grew very close to my children, Mike and Anna. We supported each other through the dark days and have continued to do so ever since. Wayne Buller, a teacher and friend, walked close to me in this time of deep need. I will always be grateful to him. I was a fellow human being who was hurting. I found that Jesus loved me just as much in my hurting state as in my successes. In fact I felt his compassion even more. He told me he loved me just as much when I was taking a nap as when I was preaching! Although to be honest, I'm still working on that one!

"This High Priest (Jesus) of ours understands our weaknesses, for he faced all of the same testings we do, yet he did not sin. [16] So let us come boldly to the throne of our gracious God. There we will receive his mercy, and we will find grace to help us when we need it most."

- Hebrews 4:15-16 NLT

Chapter 23:

He is Working All Things For Your Good

Be Transparent

It is how important to be transparent. I know as Christians sometimes we feel like we have to act like we have it all together. When we are not doing well, we should not hide or feel ashamed. It is all part of the walk. Jesus said, "In this world, you are going to have struggles" (John 16:33). We are going to have trials. It comes with living in a fallen world. Some Christians teach that because you are a believer, and living by faith, you aren't going to go through hard times. If you believe this, you will struggle with condemnation and wonder what's wrong with you when facing a trial. I always try to break that condemnation off people. I tell people that Jesus went through struggles, Paul went through struggles, I go through struggles, and you are going to go through struggles too! It's okay, we are all in this together. Thankfully, He will never leave us or forsake us! (Heb. 13:5), and we will eventually overcome!

When one person in the body of Christ is hurting, we all hurt. We are all connected. Jesus has connected us. We need to have a heart for the hurting like Jesus does. We should not harden our heart toward those people even when bad decisions have added to their problems.

One of the things that I love about Paul was that he was very transparent. He talked about a time in his life where he was so depressed he didn't even want to live: "For we do not want you to be ignorant, brethren, of our trouble which came to us in Asia; that we were burdened beyond measure, above strength, so that we despaired even of life" (2 Cor. 1:8). Paul was saying: "We got to the point where we didn't want to live. We were so depressed and barely holding on." Then he continued, "Yes, we had the sentence of death in ourselves that we should not trust in ourselves..." (v 9a). How often do we get down on ourselves when we are going through struggles? Don't we wish we had done this or that differently? We beat ourselves up, and then the enemy comes in and beats us up even more!

Paul continues saying, "We should not trust in ourselves, but trust in God who raises the dead" (v. 10b). Aren't you glad we serve a powerful God? He is much bigger than the trial you are going through, even though it may not feel that way. Paul finishes his thought, "(God) who delivered us from so great a death, and does deliver us, in whom we trust that He will still deliver us, you also help together in prayer for us, that thanks may be given by many persons on our behalf for the gift granted to us through many" (v. 10-11).

There were many times when Paul desperately needed help. Sometimes people came alongside him, but just as often they abandoned him. No matter what, the Holy Spirit was always there to help him. I love what Frances Chan says in his book *The Forgotten God:* "I don't want to just write about the Holy Spirit, I want to experience His presence in my life in a profound way so I can impact others."

We experience the profoundness of the Holy Spirit in our deepest struggles and trials, and yet we need to cheer up, because Jesus said He has overcome! (John 16:33).

Don't Isolate

God is with you no matter what you are going through. Don't allow yourself to get under condemnation, and whatever you do don't isolate yourself. Isolation is what the enemy wants to do to you. Reach out to others. I have found that being authentic takes much less energy than trying to put on a false "Pollyanna" face while going through a struggle. It is not contradictory to be honest about fear, pain or trials, yet still trust God. When you are going through a difficulty, it is important to share it with like minded believers. They will be there for you and walk with you and pray you through it. Somebody once said to me: "Fake it until you make it." I think that is a horrible saying. We don't want to fake it–we want to be real, and we will make it!

Jesus has given His life so we can take our masks off. He has forgiven us. He is with us so we can be real. It is a waste of energy to try to impress people. When we allow ourselves to be authentic in both our strengths and weaknesses, we have an opportunity to impact many, many people. I am a kinder, more compassionate person having gone through those difficulties. Have I arrived? Absolutely not. God is still working on me. I am still going for theophostic therapy once a month. I know there is a lot more I've got to learn. But, I do know that when the Holy Spirit weaves these truths and values into our hearts, He then raises us to that place where we can really help others.

Why Rejoice in Difficulties?

Both James, the half brother of Jesus, and Paul write about how we need to "rejoice" in our trials. This seems ridiculous until they go on to explain why. James says when we have a right attitude in our difficulties; we gain patience which makes us mature and complete (James 1:2-4).

Paul explains having a positive attitude in the midst of struggles not only gives us perseverance (the ability to hang in there when all strength is gone). It also produces character which gives us hope along with an extra outpouring of His love (Romans 5:3-5). This is very hard to do since our natural reaction to things going badly is to grumble and complain. Think about it. When we have a bad attitude it compounds the problem and amplifies it.

As I was writing this, something terribly unfair happened to me. It was unexpected and really ticked me off. I thought "I'm not rejoicing" and that was an understatement. I knew I had to deal with it. So I stopped writing, put on some worship music and began to thank Him for the trial. It seemed phony at first, but then everything shifted and suddenly He became bigger than the problem. I felt strength and my wife noticed how well I was handling the situation (character). I had a renewed hope that everything would work out, and I felt His unconditional love permeate my heart and the heaviness lifted. Wow, it actually worked! My attitude shocked my wife!

Trials can make us feel small and overwhelmed, but rejoicing gives us strength to go on. Whether we feel it or not, our character is becoming more like Jesus. When we get to Heaven, God will not be impressed with our accomplishments, but He will be blessed by our changed character which we will bring with us to Heaven!

We can't allow the enemy to rob us of hope. Hope is what sustains us. A person can live approximately 33 days without food, 5 days without water, and 7 minutes without oxygen, but we really can't live without hope. When we keep our eyes on God in the struggle, then He gives us hope and His love. This causes blessing for us and spills over to bless the lives of other people. So let's rejoice when trials come!

Be Sensitive to Others

It is important to be sensitive to other people going through struggles. Sometimes the Holy Spirit will come and let you know that the person you're sitting next to on an airplane, or working next to, or living next to is really going through it. I had this experience on a recent flight. I wanted to check out and sleep as it was a long flight. I didn't want to talk with the person next to me. I could sense she was going through some struggles so I decided to be friendly. It was interesting. She was an older lady that had been a Nun, and had recently become a Zen Buddhist. Isn't it amazing that in that whole plane, God put this woman next to me? She was going through a very difficult trial in her life. To be honest, I was really tired, but the Holy Spirit prompted me.

We had the most amazing conversation. I told her I had run the Monterey Zendo in California. We talked, and I had a chance to share with her about Jesus in a fresh way. When she got off that plane, she said that she couldn't tell me enough how thankful she was that she sat next to me. She was fun; she was fiery. She said that she was going to give Jesus another chance because Zen wasn't doing it for her. Sometimes, when the Holy Spirit prompts you it is not comfortable, but God had a better plan, and I am so glad I didn't sleep. I am thankful I obeyed the promptings of the Spirit. In the past I have said,

"Forget it, I am going to sleep." I may never know the consequences of not heeding the voice of Love in those moments, but I want the Holy Spirit to flow through me whenever He desires, not just when it is convenient.

Life in the Spirit is exciting! It is amazing in every way. Each day I learn new facets of this incredible God I am privileged to love and serve and walk with. I encourage you to explore all that He has for you. The Holy Spirit will empower you in ways you cannot imagine, He has gifts for you to unwrap and give away. He desires to communicate with you and impart His wisdom and revelation into your heart. He wants you whole, physically and emotionally. He wants to pray through your human spirit, speaking mysteries as you talk in tongues and are built up. And He wants to reveal Himself to you as the comforter. He will work all things together for your good. He will not let one drop of your sorrow go to waste. As you offer it to Him, He will let it bring Him glory and turn it into your joy. This is the life He always intended for you!

> *"Father, I thank you that in all the trials and struggles we go through you promise to bring good out of whatever we go through, as we love you and are called according to Your purpose. You turn everything to good because You are a good God and a loving Father. Lord, give us opportunities to minister to others the same comfort we have received. Father, I pray that for each and every one of us, You will cause your Holy Spirit to prompt, guide and lead us from a loving heart and to really make a difference in this world." In Jesus' name, Amen.*

Afterword

Life is an adventure and the Holy Spirit wants to partner with you. Life in the Spirit is meant to be free and fulfilling. It is meant to be shared since the journey has much to offer, you might as well enjoy the ride. When we get to Heaven, I pray we will hear those words we long to hear: "Well done my good and faithful servant." Until we meet in Heaven and spend eternity together:

"The Lord bless you and keep you,
The Lord make His face shine upon you,
And be gracious to you.
The Lord lift up His countenance upon you,
And give you peace."
- Numbers 6:24-26

I love you,

Contact Information:

**For speaking engagements, seminars,
men's conferences or consultation…**

jr@therock.org

(303) 688-0777 ext 206

To view JR speaking go to www.jrpolhemus.com

CPSIA information can be obtained
at www.ICGtesting.com
Printed in the USA
FSOW03n1232251016
26550FS

9 781498 486941